# Report Writing
## For Architects and Project Managers

**Also from Blackwell Science**

*The Architect in Practice*
D. Chappell & C.J. Willis
0–632–02267–1

*Building Sub-Contract Documentation*
David Chappell & Vincent Powell-Smith
0–632–02084–9

*The JCT Design and Build Contract*
David Chappell & Vincent Powell-Smith
0–632–02081–4

*Contractual Correspondence for Architects and Project Managers*
David Chappell
0–632–04002–5

*Standard Letters for Building Contractors*
David Chappell
0–632–03452–1

*Standard Letters in Architectural Practice*
David Chappell
0–632–03451–3

*In preparation*

*Causation and Delay in Construction Disputes*
Nicholas J. Carnell
0–632–03971–X

*Collateral Warranties*
Second Edition
Winward Fearon
0–632–03896–9

*The JCT Standard Form of Building Contract JCT 80*
Vincent Powell-Smith
0–632–03963–9

*Building Sub-contracts: A Guide for Specialist Contractors*
S.T. Rudi Klein
0–632–03763–6

*An Arbitration Casebook*
John Parris & Vincent Powell-Smith
0–632–03936–1

*Alternative Dispute Resolution in Construction Contracts*
Peter R. Hibberd & Paul Newman
0–632–03817–9

*EU Public Procurement Law*
David Medhurst
0–632–03813–6

# Report Writing
## For Architects and Project Managers

**Third Edition**

# David Chappell
*BA (Hons Arch), MA (Arch), MA (Law), PhD, RIBA*
Architect and Contracts Consultant
Chappell-Marshall Limited

Blackwell
Science

© David Chappell 1984, 1989, 1996 by
Blackwell Science Ltd
Editorial Offices:
Osney Mead, Oxford OX2 0EL
25 John Street, London WC1N 2BL
23 Ainslie Place, Edinburgh EH3 6AJ
238 Main Street, Cambridge
   Massachusetts 02142, USA
54 University Street, Carlton
   Victoria 3053, Australia

Other Editorial Offices:
Arnette Blackwell SA
   224, Boulevard Saint Germain
   75007 Paris, France

Blackwell Wissenschafts-Verlag GmbH
   Kurfürstendamm 57
   10707 Berlin, Germany

   Zehetnergasse 6
   A-1140 Wien
   Austria

First edition published 1984
   by The Architectural Press Ltd
Second edition published 1989
   by Legal Studies & Services Ltd
Third edition published 1996
   by Blackwell Science Ltd

Set in 10.5 Times
by DP Photosetting, Aylesbury, Bucks
Printed and bound in Great Britain by
Hartnolls Ltd, Bodmin, Cornwall

The Blackwell Science logo is a
trade mark of Blackwell Science Ltd,
registered at the United Kingdom
Trade Marks Registry

DISTRIBUTORS

Marston Book Services Ltd
PO Box 269
Abingdon
Oxon OX14 4YN
(Orders: Tel: 01235 465500
         Fax: 01235 465555)

USA
Blackwell Science, Inc.
238 Main Street
Cambridge, MA 02142
(Orders: Tel: 800 215-1000
         617 876-7000
         Fax: 617 492-5263)

Canada
Copp Clark, Ltd
2775 Matheson Blvd East
Mississauga, Ontario
Canada, L4W 4P7
(Orders: Tel: 800 263-4374
         905 238-6074)

Australia
Blackwell Science Pty Ltd
54 University Street
Carlton, Victoria 3053
(Orders: Tel: 03 9347-0300
         Fax: 03 9349-3016)

A catalogue record for this title
is available from the British Library

ISBN 0-632-04001-7

Library of Congress
Cataloging-in-Publication Data
Chappell, David.
   Report writing for architects and
project managers/David Chappell.—3rd ed.
      p. cm.
   Rev. ed. of: Report writing for
architects. London: Architectural Press;
New York: Nichols Pub. Co., 1984.
   Includes index.
   ISBN 0-632-04001-7
   1. Architectural writing.   I. Chappell,
David.   Report writing for architects.
II. Title.
NA2540.C48   1996
808'.06672—dc20                      96-5630
                                        CIP

# Contents

# Preface to the Third Edition

It is seven years since the second edition was published and many small changes of terminology in the formats have been necessary. A new edition has also given me the opportunity to enlarge on some areas where I have seen deficiencies and to make clearer some things which on reflection may have been obscure. In particular, the section dealing with contractor's claims has been expanded to give some guidance if the contractor submits a common law claim and, in response to a reviewer's request, the expert witness's duties have been included. In the last edition, attention was drawn to the confused position regarding disclaimers in reports following conflicting decisions of the Court of Appeal. Happily, both decisions were considered by the House of Lords and a summary of the conclusions is included.

The introduction of the Construction (Design and Management) Regulations 1994 (commonly referred to as the 'CDM Regulations') and the accompanying administrative problems has been a source of concern in the industry, especially to architects or project managers taking on the duties of the planning supervisor. Although not strictly a 'report', I have bowed to requests and tentatively included a format for the 'health and safety plan' to be prepared by the planning supervisor. I say tentatively because such plans are essentially unique to each project and, therefore, a format can only be considered to be an elementary checklist. I am indebted to my colleague Michael J. Cowlin LLB(Hons), DipOSH, ACIArb, Barrister, for this part of the text.

I hope that users of this book will find it more useful than before. I have tried to retain the essential purpose of the book – to provide a set of formats to act as simple guides for architects and project managers preparing reports.

David Chappell 1996
Chappell-Marshall Limited
27 Westgate
Tadcaster
North Yorkshire
LS24 9JB

# Introduction

A report is an account given or an opinion which is expressed formally on the basis of investigation or consideration. The keywords in that definition are 'formally' and 'investigation'. A report should be set out in a particular way, with headings and sub-headings, so as to present your findings as clearly as possible.

Report writing appears to be a much neglected branch of architectural practice; something to be 'picked up' as the architect matures. This is a strange situation because a sizeable portion of the architect's work consists of preparing reports of one sort or another. Report formats vary considerably from office to office. At one extreme, they are bound in expensive covers and presented as compendiums of notes, drawings and photographs; at the other, they take the form of long letters, perhaps with addenda. A common practice is to dig out a similar report to the one you are preparing and follow the general lines. If a similar report is not available, the content has to be developed from first principles.

This volume brings together standard report formats to cover all the common, and one or two less common, examples. It is hoped that, by following the formats set out and making use of the checklists, the architect's job will be simplified. In addition some general notes have been included to highlight important points but no attempt has been made to deal with report writing from first principles and thus duplicate the many excellent books which deal in considerable detail with report writing for all purposes.

My thanks go to the many people who have contributed helpful suggestions and advice, and to Caroline Dalziel who undertook the proof reading. In particular, I wish to thank my wife, Margaret, for restraint in the face of my constant scribbling.

For convenience, the male pronoun has been used throughout. 'He' may be taken to mean 'he' or 'she'.

*Further reading*
*Writing Technical Reports*, Cooper, B.M., Harmondsworth, 1964, Penguin.

*The Art of Readable Writing*, Flesch, R., London, 1962, Collier-Macmillan.

*Plain Words*, Gowers, Sir Ernest, London, 1948, HMSO.

*ABC of Plain Words*, Gowers, Sir Ernest, London, 1951, HMSO.

*Writing Matters*, Hamilton, A., London, 1989, RIBA.

*Technical Report Writing Today*, Pauley, S.E. & Riordan, D.G., 1995, Houghton Mifflin.

*Reports and How to Write Them*, Shearing, H.A., London, 1965, Allen & Unwin.

*Good English: How to Write It*, Vallins, G.H., London, 1951, Pan.

*Writing, Researching, Communicating*, Windschuttle, K. & Elliott, E., 1993, McGraw-Hill.

# 1 Terms of Reference

Because this is a book about report writing, it is considered appropriate that the book itself should begin by stating its own terms of reference.

- ❑ It is intended to provide a set of formats to assist architects and surveyors to produce good reports for their clients.
- ❑ It is assumed that, although the architect using this book may not be skilled at writing reports, he will be skilled at his own job and in finding the information which will go into the report.
- ❑ The book is not intended as a guide for the writing of reports by anyone for any occasion although, undoubtedly, much of the information which follows will be generally useful.
- ❑ Every major circumstance which could generate a report in connection with architectural practice has been included. Several less common types of report are also covered.
- ❑ One final, and I hope not unreasonable, assumption has been made: that the architect is capable of writing good clear concise English. I have tried to do just that in the text which follows.

# 2 The Report

## 2.1 Purpose

Before setting pen to paper, it is essential to ask yourself why you are writing the report. There are only three possibilities:

- ❏ You are giving information
- ❏ You are seeking information
- ❏ You are seeking decisions or approvals

Usually, a report is a combination of all three. Do not fall into the habit of producing a report if a short letter will do. Conversely, always write a clearly set out report rather than a long rambling letter.

## 2.2 Who will read?

When writing anything, you must always bear in mind your prospective reader. Are you preparing your report for the benefit of other professionals in the construction industry? I use the term 'professional' in its loosest sense to encompass all those who might be said to have some kind of expert knowledge of the processes involved. If you are writing for this audience, then it is perfectly reasonable – indeed it is probably desirable – to make full use of the normal phraseology of construction, which shortens the report because there is no need for detailed explanations. Similarly, if your report is being prepared for the benefit of a solicitor, it is reasonable to suppose that he does not expect you to explain the implications of liquidated damages and similar provisions.

Very often, however, you will be writing for the benefit of business people or laymen. Your client is likely to be a layman in terms of the construction industry. In such cases your report must be written so as to be easily understandable without any technical knowledge. If a technical point has to be included, it must be explained clearly. A glossary of terms at the end of the report is generally an irritant to be avoided. If in doubt, or if your report is likely to be read by professionals and laymen, always write for the layman. It is an elementary point, but frequently overlooked.

Your report may be read by large numbers of people with different interests in the content. The motives of the readers may sometimes conflict, some being committed to seeing the project reach fruition, others looking for reasons to bring it to an end. A large company which is trying to decide whether to build new premises or to buy an existing building and convert may well commission a report on the options. This could take the form of a report on development possibilities together with an inspection of property (Sections 5.1 and 5.2). In such circumstances, it should be borne in mind that there are likely to be factions within the company who have their own reasons for favouring one solution over the other. How you deal with this will depend on your own skill in client relations, but it will certainly affect the tone of your report. If working for one person, you must be aware which criteria are uppermost in his or her mind and shape your report accordingly. It is not a question of what to leave out, that is a dangerous game to play, but of where to place the emphasis.

Finally, always avoid the use of jargon. It tends to be the last resort of those with nothing much to say.

## 2.3   Format

Working to a plan simplifies any job. This is particularly true of report writing. The use of report formats should save time and avoid mistakes as they enable the mind to be freed from the routine part of the task to concentrate on the important aspects. Reports can be considered in two ways:

❏   What to write
❏   How to write it

If the 'how' can be set out in a particular pattern, like a railway line with a choice of stations at which to stop, the 'what' becomes much easier, being signalled by each station.

All the report formats in this book are arranged in a particular pattern. The main headings are listed in logical sequence, and under each heading there is a series of sub-headings. A selection of useful paragraphs and checklists is given under each sub-heading, together with descriptive material where neither the specific paragraph nor checklists are appropriate. It should be remembered, however, that the formats are not an alternative to using your own words and imparting your own distinctive style. The system of numbering enables additional paragraphs to be added without difficulty.

Clearly, not every heading, paragraph or item on the checklists will be applicable. It is also inevitable that your report will contain some features relative to a particular project. However, by reading through the formats when preparing a report it should be possible to produce a competent report with minimum delay and to concentrate effort where it is most needed.

When writing any formal work such as a book or dissertation, it is usual to structure it as follows:

❑ Title page
❑ Table of contents
❑ List of illustrations
❑ Acknowledgements
❑ Introduction
❑ Text
❑ Bibliography
❑ Appendices
❑ Index

If a preface is used, it is normally placed immediately before the table of contents. It is useful to bear in mind this structure if you are called upon to produce a report which is not covered by the formats in this book. Most reports, however, do not warrant such elaborate treatment and the formats which follow are based upon a much simpler structure:

❑ Title page
❑ Table of contents
❑ Introduction
❑ Summary
❑ Text
❑ Appendices

It is suggested that acknowledgements and bibliography, where they exist at all, form such a small part of the report that they can be included as part of the appendices. It is not usual to include an index, but there may be occasions when an index is useful. An obvious example would be if the report was long or complex.

## 2.4  Presentation

It is well worth while giving considerable thought to the appearance of
your report. Although the actual materials and style will vary according to your taste, certain things are essential in all reports.

Some firms have a standard cover and backing sheet so that all their
reports are immediately recognisable. This creates a good impression,
and it helps to have the practice name, address and telephone number
preprinted on the cover, with the word REPORT in large letters. It
may be expensive to maintain large stocks of such covers, but standard
covers, without the word REPORT, can be useful for other purposes,
for example practice information or periodic newsletters. In this way,
all the office literature will have a co-ordinated image.

The client's name, the subject of the report and your own name and
date should be contained on the title sheet, followed by a contents list.
Even if the report is relatively short a contents list simplifies the job of
finding a particular item quickly. For this reason it is essential to start
each new section on a new page unless the report is very short.

You will have your own ideas about the layout of the text on the
page and it is not the purpose of this book to attempt to impose any
particular style or design. There are, however, some points worth
keeping in mind:

- [ ] Leave generous margins, particularly near the spine. It assists in
  binding and your clients will find the space useful for pencilling in
  any points they wish to raise with you.
- [ ] Your principal aim will be to present the contents of your report
  effectively whether putting an argument, stating facts or requesting
  decisions. The best way is through clarity of expression. Clear
  numbering, of pages, of sections and of paragraphs will help.
- [ ] Some people prefer to double-space the type, but it is not strictly
  necessary if you leave adequate margins. The combination of
  double spacing and generous margins tends to produce an unneces-
  sarily bulky report while giving sparse information on each page.
  One and a half spacing is a good compromise.
- [ ] Notes and references should be avoided if possible. They are
  irritating and interrupt the flow of the text. If they are unavoid-
  able, such as when a fact must be proven, they can be put in any of
  three positions: as footnotes; sidenotes (in the margin); or end-
  notes. There are special, rather complex rules involved here and
  you should consult one of the books which deal with the subject.
  Once again it is important to consider who will read the report. An
  academic will appreciate footnotes, the business person may not.

Relegate any additional information (such as drawings, photographs, tables and statistics) to the appendices. The exception to this is when you are referring to defects. Here, a photograph of the defect can be usefully included as part of the text with arrows, etc. stuck on.

Some architects prefer to include tables and graphs within the text. Although, in general, this is to be avoided because it makes the report unwieldy and difficult to follow, a table has great value in briefly presenting large quantities of information. Therefore, a table, graph, histogram or the like is to be preferred if it can replace (not merely supplement) several pages of text. However, you should not allow more than one page of photographs, tables, etc. at a time to occur within the text, because the reader will soon lose the thread of any argument if it is interrupted by the need to study illustrations.

Any plans which you think it necessary to include in the appendices should be either A4 format or folded in such a way that they can be easily opened clear of the report when it is closed. If a particular plan or set of plans is very bulky, you can put them in an envelope formed inside the back cover. However, this practice should be avoided if possible because it makes the report difficult to handle.

It is becoming increasingly common for the architect to give an elaborate presentation to his client in the form of slides, tapes and videos. Although such devices and your sheer enthusiasm may create a favourable impression, it is the report which will remain as tangible evidence of your endeavours after the visual/aural presentation is over. In such instances, the report layout should be devised to trigger memories of the aural presentation, but the content of the report must be capable of standing alone.

Finally, make sure that the report is properly bound so that it can be opened flat. A comparative analysis of the common methods of binding (as shown in Table 2.1 over) may be of some use here.

## 2.5   Summary of main points

- ❏ If feasible, write a short letter rather than a report.
- ❏ Write a report rather than long letter.
- ❏ Write report for professionals or laymen as required.
- ❏ Avoid jargon.
- ❏ Use formats to save time and avoid mistakes.
- ❏ Have a standard cover.
- ❏ Have a contents list.

❏   Have an appendix.
❏   Bind to open flat.
❏   Plans should be A4 or easily openable.
❏   The report should be part of overall presentation.

**Table 2.1**   Binding methods

| Binding | Advantages | Disadvantages |
|---|---|---|
| Plastic spiral | Opens flat<br>Relatively cheap<br>Good appearance | Can tear the paper<br>Requires special machine<br>Requires generous margins<br>Can become tangled |
| Plastic clip spine | Cheap<br>Easy to apply | Difficult to open flat<br>Pages become detached |
| Folding staples and bar | Cheap<br>Easy to apply | Difficult to open flat<br>Untidy appearance<br>Steel can cause cuts |
| Staple, washer and single hole | Cheap<br>Easy to apply | Poor appearance<br>Steel can cause cuts |
| Staples and plastic binding | Cheap<br>Easy to apply | Difficult to open flat<br>Unsuitable for thick reports |
| Ring binder | Good appearance<br>Opens flat<br>Relatively cheap<br>Easy to apply | Requires generous margins<br>Can tear the paper |
| Glued spine and plastic binding | Good appearance<br>Margins not critical<br>Opens flat | Not cheap<br>Pages can detach with use |
| Fully sewn, glued and bound | Good appearance<br>Margins not critical | Expensive<br>Requires professional techniques |

# 3 Content

## 3.1 Fact and opinion

The content of the report will be divided into facts and opinion. It is very important to make the distinction very clear, particularly if the report may be used in legal proceedings (in practice, this means every report you write).

The collection of facts must always be placed first in any particular section of the report. It is common for the factual content of any report to represent well over 65% of the whole. In the case of feasibility reports, inspections and surveys, fact may represent 90% of the entire document.

'Fact' means exactly that; actual incontrovertible statements relating to the existing situation at a particular time – the condition of a building for example, or the actual state of a job in progress. It is perfectly acceptable to include as a statement of fact the statement that the planning authority 'appear to have no objections'. However, this is quite different from stating that 'I do not consider that the planning authority will have any objections' and you should recognise the difference. The first is a statement of fact; the second is an opinion.

Opinions should be collected together and included in a conclusion. In addition, there may well be other sections which are largely opinion, such as a description of a proposed design or the financial viability of a project. However, do avoid scattering opinions throughout the report. Not only is it difficult to read and digest them but the report becomes less convincing if early opinions form the basis of later conclusions.

The report should build up in a totally comprehensible way from a collection of facts to a series of opinions and conclusions based upon the facts. Too often reports are produced after much labour, care is taken in the presentation and they are sent to a client without any response being received. On inquiry, your client may say that he thought the report was simply for information. Remember that most reports must end with a question to ensure a follow up. The question may request instructions, decisions or simply an approval for the course of action you are suggesting. In practice, you will find that it

is not always easy to stick rigidly to such counsel of perfection, but you
should make every endeavour to do so.

Some people like to have a summary of the main points of a report
right at the beginning so that they can get a grasp of what the report
contains immediately. Arguments in favour of a summary are:

❑   It is invaluable for the reader who has little time
❑   It informs the dedicated reader what to expect in the main body of
    the report

The argument against a summary flows from the arguments in favour.
It may, paradoxically, ensure that fewer people read the main body of
the report and, thus, overlook many important points. Once again, you
must consider for whom the report is intended. If you are dealing with
a client who in reality comprises a board of directors with an input of
opinion from many departmental managers, a summary is likely to be
essential. Indeed, there is a strong argument for producing what
amounts to special condensed versions of the report in such circumstances. Beware, however; a condensed report must always be clearly
labelled as such or complications can arise. Just what is required is a
matter between you and your client.

The formats in this book assume that a summary is required. It is
usual to put it immediately after the introduction or to have a special
summary sheet inside the front cover. Each summary will be a unique
piece of writing. It is usual to incorporate briefly in a summary all the
conclusions and decisions required. For this reason, some architects
dispense with a summary and put the conclusions first. It offends logic
to take this approach.

## 3.2   Style

The actual style of writing will vary with the individual but you should
aim at a crisp and clear presentation of your information. A chatty
approach which may be quite suitable in a letter to your client is quite
inappropriate in a formal report. Do not be afraid to subdivide
sections in the interests of clarity. Avoid excessive cross-referencing
which can become irritating.

When you state your opinion or conclusions make it absolutely clear
that they are simply your opinions. Do not adopt an apologetic style
and do not ramble on long after you have made your point. Build your
arguments carefully, indicating your reasoning where appropriate. If
the facts speak for themselves, your conclusion may be one sentence.

Advice should also be part of your conclusion, for example: 'Therefore, the only viable course of action appears to be total demolition'.

Be prepared to spend time in drafting your report. The act of writing concentrates the mind wonderfully. In the first draft, you will decide just what you need to include. It is at this stage that the formats will be found most useful. The second draft will be concerned with expressing the contents in the best possible way. Do not be surprised if you need a third or fourth draft before you achieve a report which exactly expresses what you want to say. You may find that your final draft has departed considerably from the format from which you started. That does not matter. By that stage the format has served its purpose.

Finally, do allocate sufficient time to carefully read your report, editing out loose phrases and checking grammar, punctuation and spelling. Nothing will lose you the confidence of your client more than a badly arranged, poorly typed, misspelt initial report – no matter that it is bound in the finest leather.

## 3.3  Summary of main points

- ❏  Put facts first.
- ❏  Put opinions, deduced from facts, in the conclusion.
- ❏  Advice should be included as part of the conclusion.
- ❏  End with a question to ensure a follow up.
- ❏  A summary may be put after the introduction or as a separate sheet inside the cover.
- ❏  Avoid cross-referencing.
- ❏  Be clear and brief.
- ❏  A good report needs many drafts.
- ❏  Check grammar, punctuation and spelling.

# 4 Reports Associated with Building Projects

## 4.1 Feasibility

This type of report is produced as part of stage B of the RIBA Plan of Work.

After you have prepared the brief in consultation with your client, the most important consideration is whether the project is feasible. On very small works of alteration, a formal report may be unnecessary. It may be quite clear that the work can proceed. Care is needed because the size of job is not the key factor. It is suggested that, even on small works, the format which follows should be used as a checklist. It is all too easy to overlook something which could spell disaster. Working through the format is a useful discipline on every project whether or not you decide that a formal report is required.

The purpose of a feasibility report to your clients is to assemble into one package all the criteria which must be taken into account so that they can make the important decision about proceeding with the project. At this early stage, it is difficult to decide exactly what data will be strictly relevant. If in doubt, it is wisest to include rather than exclude information. There are some factors which must always receive attention, such as the cost implications of alternative approaches and the likely position with regard to statutory approvals. Your clients' decision will be influenced by the skill with which you correlate the information in order to present them with reasonable options.

Clearly, the feasibility report required for a small project will be quite different from a report dealing with a large complex on a city centre site. The difference, however, is mainly a matter of quantity of information and presentation. The general pattern of the report should be the same in both cases.

# *FEASIBILITY REPORT FORMAT*

**Client**
**Project title**
**Feasibility report**
**Date**

**Table of contents**

**1   Introduction**

1.1   In accordance with your instructions of the [*insert date*] I submit for your consideration my feasibility report on the [*insert name of project*].

1.2   **Summary**

**2   Terms of reference** [*include items as appropriate*]

2.1   [*Give short outline of brief received from client*]

2.2   It will be appreciated that the report has been prepared within a very short period of time. It has not been possible to investigate thoroughly the potential of the site/existing property [*omit as appropriate*]. The contents, however, should enable basic policy decisions to be made. A fully comprehensive report can be prepared later, if required, after a closer investigation of all relevant factors has been carried out.

2.3   A full measured survey of the site/existing property [*omit as appropriate*] has/has not [*omit as appropriate*] been carried out. See separate report [*omit as appropriate*].

2.4   A structural analysis has/has not [*omit as appropriate*] been carried out. Therefore, certain assumptions have had to be made pending future investigation [*omit as appropriate*].

2.5   The precise site boundaries have yet to be established.

2.6   No soil investigation has been carried out and the report is based on the assumption that ground-bearing and water conditions will prove suitable for building purposes without excessive costs.

2.7   Sketch plans indicate possibilities in the broadest terms.

2.8   The following consultants and authorities have been involved
      in the preparation of this report.
      *2.8.1 Consultants*
         Quantity surveyor: [*name*]
         Structural engineer: [*name*]
         Geotechnical engineer: [*name*]
         Electrical engineer: [*name*]
         Heating and ventilation engineer: [*name*]
         Mechanical engineer: [*name*]
         Acoustics: [*name*]
         Landscape architect:[*name*]
         Others: [*name*]
      *2.8.2 Authorities*
         Planning: [*name*]
         Highways: [*name*]
         Drainage: [*name*]
         Housing: [*name*]
         Education: [*name*]
         Fire brigade: [*name*]
         Transport: [*name*]
         British Coal: [*area*]
         Electricity: [*area*]
         Nuclear Electric: [*area*]
         National Power: [*area*]
         Powergen: [*area*]
         Water: [*area*]
         Gas: [*area*]
         British Telecom: [*area*]
         Police: [*area*]
         Forestry Commission: [*area*]
         National Trust: [*area*]
         Royal Fine Arts Commission
         English Heritage.

2.9   At the time of preparation of this report it had not proved
      possible to consult the following:
         [*list*]
      Information given is, to the best of my knowledge, correct.
      However, it will be appreciated that until formal procedures
      are concluded (e.g. planning application and negotiation with
      other authorities), certain parts of this report must be consid-
      ered as the best information available at the present time as a
      result of personal interviews with the appropriate officials.

**3   General information** [*include items as appropriate*]

3.1   **Site location**
[*Describe the location of the site or property in relation to:*
❑   *distance from nearest urban centre*
❑   *topography of the land including notes on existing walls, fences, hedges, trees and buildings*
❑   *nearby rivers, streams or watercourses, danger of flooding*
❑   *ownership and use of adjoining land or property*
❑   *possible nuisances (e.g. factories, airports, motorways)*]

3.2   **Access**
*3.2.1  Bus services*
The following principal bus services are available from:
[*Insert place and distance away*]
[*List main services and regularity*]
*3.2.2  Train services*
The following principal train services are available from:
[*Insert place and distance away*]
[*List main services and regularity*]
*3.2.3  Air services*
The following air services are available from:
[*Insert place and distance away*]
[*List main services and regularity*]
*3.2.4  Private motorist*
The site lies within [*insert number*] miles of the M [*insert number*] motorway exit [*insert exit number*].
Other readily accessible centres are:
[*name of town or city*] – [*insert number*] miles away.

3.3   **Shopping**
Daily shopping needs are well provided for by a number of small shops strategically located.
Mobile shops call at regular intervals.
There are few shops within 1 mile radius.
The nearest large shopping centre is [*insert number*] miles away at [*insert place*].
There is an open market at [*insert place*] on [*insert days*].

3.4   **Health**
Provision for community health is as follows:
Doctors' surgeries at [*insert places*]
Dental surgeries at [*insert places*]
Opticians at [*insert places*]
Chiropodists at [*insert places*]

Clinic at [*insert place*]
Health centre at [*insert place*]
Comprehensive hospital facilities are provided at [*place and distance away*]
Further provision of [*describe provision*] within the next [*insert number*] years is expected at [*insert place*].

### 3.5 Social and recreational
Facilities are available as follows:
Public houses: [*insert place and distance*]
Hotels: [*insert place and distance*]
WMC: [*insert place and distance*]
Swimming baths: [*insert place and distance*]
Leisure centre: [*insert place and distance*]
Cricket club: [*insert place and distance*]
Football club: [*insert place and distance*]
Rugby club: [*insert place and distance*]
Angling club: [*insert place and distance*]
Sailing club: [*insert place and distance*]
Community centre: [*insert place and distance*]
Library: [*insert place and distance*]
Art gallery: [*insert place and distance*]
Museum: [*insert place and distance*]
Places of worship:
Anglican: [*insert place and distance*]
Roman Catholic: [*insert place and distance*]
Methodist: [*insert place and distance*]
Baptist: [*insert place and distance*]
Others:
[*Include any other clubs or social centres nearby*].

### 3.6 Education
The following schools are available:
[*insert place, distance, state, private, mixed or single-sex for each school*]
Nursery/play groups
5–9 years old
9–13 years old
13–16 years old
Sixth form college
Further education.
Further provision of [*describe*] within the next [*insert number*] years is expected at [*insert places*].

### 3.7 Employment
The major employers in the area are:

[*List employers, nature of business, place and distance from the site*].
In addition, there is a wide range of minor employers: [*Describe*].
There are, at present, no major employers in the area.

## 4 Factors affecting the scheme
[*Include items as appropriate*]

### 4.1 Rights
Of light: [*describe*]
Of way: [*describe*]
Of support: [*describe*]
Party walls: [*describe*]
Easements: [*describe*]
Covenants: [*describe*]
Other: [*describe*].

### 4.2 Planning constraints
*4.2.1* The planning authority has raised no objection to the development in principle.

*4.2.2* A previous expired/unexpired [*omit as appropriate*] planning permission was granted for [*describe*].

*4.2.3* The following conditions are expected to be applied to any future approval:
[*List standard conditions and any conditions the planning authority has led you to believe will be imposed on this project*].

*4.2.4* The following planning requirements are applicable to this project:
Storey heights: [*specify*]
Number of storeys: [*specify*]
Densities: [*specify*]
Access: [*specify*]
Materials: [*specify*]
Parking: [*specify*]
Other: [*specify*].

*4.2.5* Planning permission has been given for [*describe the nature of the development*] on a piece of land/for buildings [*omit as appropriate and describe the relationship to the site*].

*4.2.6* Provisional building lines have been orally agreed as follows:
[*Road or street name*] – [*distance in metres*].

*4.2.7* An improvement line will be required to [*insert name of road or street*] as shown on the site plan in the appendices.

*4.2.8* [*Include any other road diversion or closure or planning proposal which may have an effect on the site*]

*4.2.9* Full planning approval will be required in due course.

*4.2.10* It is thought that planning approval will not be required.

*4.2.11* The scheme must comply with the Building Regulations and the appropriate notices must be submitted in due course.

4.3 **Licensing approvals**

*4.3.1* Approval will be required from the licensing justices.

4.4 **Drainage**

It is not anticipated that there will be any problems in draining the site.

It is anticipated that there may be problems in draining the site [*describe the problems*].

Resolution of the problems could be achieved by [*describe possible solutions*].

4.5 **Architectural/historical considerations**

The site/building [*omit as appropriate*] is situated in a designated conservation area and special care will be required at design stage to obtain planning approval.

The building is listed grade [*insert grade*] and special care will be required at design stage to obtain planning approval.

The existing building is in a conservation area/listed grade [*insert grade or omit as appropriate*] and approval will be required for demolition. Preliminary discussions with the planning authority suggest that such approval will/will not [*omit as appropriate*] be given.

The existing building is not listed but it has some interesting aspects which should be retained if possible:

[*list*].

The proposals may be considered sensitive and opposed by local amenity societies. Consideration should be given to the best way of dealing with possible objections to avoid a public inquiry.

4.6 **Geological considerations**

Available geological information suggests that no unusual precautions will have to be taken at foundation level.

A fault/series of faults [*omit as appropriate*] run(s) across the site which will impose constraints upon the layout of the project.

The mining position is [*describe*]. It is considered that all ground settlement has ceased/ground lowering will take place [*omit as appropriate*] but, provided adequate precautions are taken, the project can proceed.

4.7 **Statutory undertakings and other services**
All normal services are available to the site.

All normal services are available to the site except [*specify*]. There may be difficulty in overcoming this problem/there should be no insurmountable difficulty in overcoming the problem [*omit as appropriate*].

Diversion of [*specify service or main*] will be required which could prove expensive.

Easements must be negotiated for the [*specify*] service.

The electricity supplier will require a sub-station within the site boundary.

The standard procedure for providing street lighting is [*indicate local street lighting procedure*].

[*Add any other information which might affect the project such as high-voltage cables over or under the site, government pipelines, complex existing installations etc.*]

4.8 **Central government policy**
[*State whether the project is in accordance with central government policy, against it, or not applicable. Give brief details and refer to statistics in appendices*]

4.9 **Local authority policy**
[*State whether the project is in accordance with local authority policy, against it, or not applicable. Give brief details and refer to statistics in appendices*]

4.10 **Grant aid**
It is expected that some/substantial [*omit as appropriate*] grant aid may be obtainable from some or all of the following sources: [*list appropriate sources*].

It is not expected that any grant aid will be obtainable for this project.

4.11 **Structural analysis**
The existing structure appears to be adequate for the purposes of realising this project.

The existing structure appears to be inadequate for the purposes of realising this project without further strengthening/replacement [*omit as appropriate*].

Some constructional techniques may have to be adopted to avoid damage to neighbouring property.

4.12  **Site access**

Access to the site is possible at the following points: [*describe with any comments necessary*].

5  **Design possibilities** [*include items as appropriate*]

5.1  [*Principal planning options, effect of site and other constraints*]

5.2  [*Principal structural options*]

5.3  [*Principal design options, effect of architectural/historical and other constraints*]

5.4  [*Principal heating and fuel options*]

6  **Phasing possibilities** [*include if appropriate*]

6.1  [*Set out phasing possibilities in relation to options in 5 above*]

7  **Estimate of cost**

7.1  [*Produce a separate estimate for each of the options and phasing in 5 and 6 above. Keep brief*]

| | |
|---|---|
| Building contract | £ |
| Additional works [*investigations, supplementary contracts etc.*] | £ |
| Direct works [*furniture, works of art etc.*] | £ |
| Fees and expenses | |
| Architect | £ |
| Quantity surveyor | £ |
| Other consultants | £ |
| Additional items (clerk of works etc.) | £ |
| TOTAL | £ |

7.2  [*Do not attempt to give maintenance and running costs or viability appraisal unless specially requested*]

7.3  It should be appreciated that the cost figures can only be considered to be very approximate at this stage and for general guidance only. The estimate is based upon rates and prices current at the date of this report. No allowance has been made for inflation and the estimate is exclusive of value-added tax (VAT).

8  **Design team programme**

8.1  On the assumption that firm decisions, approvals and instructions to proceed are given by [*insert date*], the work of the design team would normally take [*insert number*] months, producing an estimated start on site on [*insert date*].

**9   Conclusions**

9.1   [*Assessment of options in brief and recommended best option*]

9.2   **Approvals/decisions**

    *9.2.1* Your approval is requested to option [*state number*] as assessed in 9.1 above including the provisional cost estimate in 7 above. [*Add any other approvals required*]

    *9.2.2* I should be pleased to have your decision on the following matters:

        [*list decisions required, in order of priority*].

**Appendices** [*include items as appropriate*]

A   Location plan
B   Site plan [*including improvement lines, services etc.*]
C   Old site plan [*if appropriate*]
D   Geological report and plans [*if available*]
E   Mining report and plans [*if appropriate*]
F   Statistics [*if appropriate*]
G   Aerial and other photographs of the site
H   Any other information
I    Bibliography
J   Diagrammatic proposals [*if appropriate*].

## 4.2   Outline proposals

After the feasibility report has been produced and a course of action agreed with the client, outline proposals are normally produced as part of stage C of the RIBA plan of work. Outline proposals comprise a sketch design showing the disposition of the elements of the scheme together with a brief report.

It often happens that you have produced more than one scheme, each of which provides an adequate solution of the client's problems. Do not be tempted to present several schemes. He will find it difficult enough to understand and discuss one scheme. Your job is to present the best possible scheme to your client, one which you can advise him to accept. The correct point at which to resolve the kind of major decisions which could give rise to totally different schemes is at feasibility. If you present two different schemes at this stage, it suggests that you have not put the important options to your client at the right time.

If the project is small, this report may be combined with the feasibility report or with the scheme design report (Section 4.3).

# OUTLINE PROPOSALS REPORT FORMAT

**Client**
**Project title**
**Outline proposals**
**Date**

**Table of contents**

### 1 Introduction

1.1 In accordance with your instructions of the [*insert date*] I submit for your consideration my outline proposals [*insert name of project*].

1.2 **Summary**

### 2 Terms of reference [*include items as appropriate*]

2.1 The brief is set out in general terms in the feasibility report prepared on the [*insert date*]. I confirm instructions to modify the brief as follows:
[*insert short details of the modifications received, with dates – this may be particularly important later if you try to claim additional fees*].

2.2 A full measured survey of the site/existing property [*omit as appropriate*] has been carried out and it is the subject of a separate report.

2.3 A structural analysis has been carried out which indicates [*state the situation*].

2.4 Soil investigations have been carried out and indicate [*state the situation*].

2.5 Soil investigations have not yet been carried out and this report is based on the assumption that ground-bearing and water

conditions will prove suitable for building purposes without
excessive cost. [*This is a dangerous assumption at this stage,
because the scheme may founder if there are severe ground
problems*]

2.6   The following consultants and authorities have been involved
      in the preparation of this report:
      *2.6.1 Consultants*
         Quantity surveyor: [*name*]
         Structural engineer: [*name*]
         Geotechnical engineer: [*name*]
         Electrical engineer: [*name*]
         Heating and ventilation engineer: [*name*]
         Mechanical engineer: [*name*]
         Acoustics: [*name*]
         Landscape architect: [*name*]
         Others: [*name*].
      *2.6.2 Authorities*
         Planning: [*name*]
         Highways: [*name*]
         Drainage: [*name*]
         Housing: [*name*]
         Education: [*name*]
         Fire brigade: [*name*]
         Transport: [*name*]
         British Coal: [*area*]
         Electricity: [*area*]
         Nuclear Electric: [*area*]
         National Power: [*area*]
         Powergen: [*area*]
         Water: [*area*]
         Gas: [*area*]
         British Telecom: [*area*]
         Police: [*area*]
         Forestry Commission: [*area*]
         National Trust: [*area*]
         Royal Fine Arts Commission
         English Heritage.

2.7   At the time of preparation of this report it had not proved
      possible to consult the following:
         [*list*]
      Information given is, to the best of my knowledge, correct.
      However, it will be appreciated that until formal procedures
      are concluded (e.g. planning application and negotiation with

other authorities), certain parts of this report must be considered as the best information available at the present time as a result of personal interviews with the appropriate officials.

**3    Proposals** [*include items as appropriate*]

3.1    The proposals are indicated on the drawings in broad outline.

3.2    The factors affecting the scheme are set out in the feasibility report item 4.
[*If appropriate, add the following*] Further items have become apparent as follows: [*describe*].

3.3    **Scheme analysis**
Design philosophy [*general arrangement, relationship of spaces, relationship to surrounding environment, heights, widths, general appearance*].
Siting [*considerations, topography, views, orientation, flooding, noise, other pollution, visibility, other*].
Access [*off-road, rail, canal, other*].
Structure [*reinforced concrete, pre- or post-stressed concrete, steel frame, timber frame, loadbearing brick or block, other*].
Materials [*roof, walls, internal finishes, external finishes, general*].
Heating [*solid fuel, electricity, gas, solar, other – warm air, radiator, underfloor, ceiling panel, other*].
Lighting [*tungsten, fluorescent, flood, spot, other*].
Special treatments [*acoustic, thermal, sound, fire, other*].
Special installations [*lift, ventilation, kitchen, laboratory, fire prevention, provision for disabled, other*].
Special constraints [*particular factors for which provision has to be made – statutory undertakings, special equipment, planning requirements, rights, other*].
Other special considerations [*garaging, parking, site area, ministry criteria*].

**4    Phasing** [*include items as appropriate*]

4.1    The scheme does not allow for phasing. It is assumed that the project will be carried out in one operation.

4.2    If it is desired to carry out the project in more than one operation, further consideration must be given to the possibility of phasing. The following points must be taken into account:
4.2.1    Effect upon your occupation/operations [*describe*].
4.2.2    Effect upon the total cost of the project [*describe*].
4.2.3    Effect upon the total time scale of the project [*describe*].

4.2.4 Effect upon sub-contractors [*describe*].
4.2.5 Effect upon suppliers [*describe*].
4.2.6 Effect upon materials [*describe*].
4.2.7 Effect upon related projects [*describe*].
4.2.8 Planning authority, fire brigade, statutory and other related provisions [*describe*].
4.2.9 Other considerations [*describe*].

4.3   The scheme has been designed to be carried out in [*insert number*] phases as follows:
      Stage 1 [*describe*]
      Stage 2 [*describe*] etc.
      The following points must be borne in mind:
      [*as 4.2.1 to 4.2.9 above*].

**5   Estimate of cost** [*prepared in co-operation with other members of the design team*]

5.1   [*Related to phasing, if any, in 4 above*]
      Building contract                                     £
      Additional works [*investigations,
          supplementary contracts etc.*]                    £
      Direct works [*furniture, works of art etc.*]         £
      Fees and expenses
          Architect                                         £
          Quantity surveyor                                 £
          Other consultants                                 £
      Additional items (clerk of works etc.)                £ _____
      TOTAL                                                 £ _____

5.2   **Total allocated to phases**
      Stage 1                                               £
      Stage 2                                               £ _____
      TOTAL                                                 £ _____

      [*An alternative would be to split the items in 5.1 according to phasing to produce a breakdown in each phase*]

5.3   Although the figures are more accurate than the costs suggested in the feasibility report, they are still only approximate at this stage. More accurate costings will be possible when the scheme design has been completed. The estimate is based upon rates and prices current at the date of this report. No allowance has been made for inflation and the estimate is exclusive of value-added tax (VAT).

**6   Conclusions** [*include items as appropriate*]

6.1   [*Appraisal of the outline proposal in brief*]

6.2   **Approvals/decisions**
      *6.2.1* Your approval is requested to the proposals contained in this report including the details in 3 above, the phasing proposals in 4 above and the estimate of cost in 5 above.
      *6.2.2* Your instructions are requested:
      To proceed with the scheme design stage of this project.
      To initiate soil investigation procedures as an immediate next stage.
      To submit for outline planning approval.
      To submit for [*indicate other submissions*].
      Other.
      *6.2.3* Other decisions required [*specify*].

6.3   In order to achieve the tentative dates set out in the feasibility report, item 8, [*or refer to another date*] the approvals/decisions/instructions requested in this report should be communicated to me by the [*insert date*].

**Appendices**
A   Schedule of accommodation and room sizes
B   Location plan
C   Site plan
D   Proposal drawings
E   Montage photographs of block model on site
F   Perspective sketches.


# 4.3   Scheme design

This type of report is produced as part of stage D of the RIBA plan of work.

Very small projects sometimes omit the outline proposals report. Normally, however, the scheme design is presented with carefully prepared drawings showing the inter-relationship of spaces, sections and elevations in considerable detail, together with perspectives, a model and a report.

The purpose of this report is to help to explain the scheme. Therefore, many of the items included in the feasibility report have no place here and are simply incorporated by reference. The report, together with the drawings, should give clients a very clear picture of what they will be getting. Indeed, the report, once approved, can be a very useful first stage in the production of the building specification and a vital document for reference for all production information.

---

# SCHEME DESIGN FORMAT

---

**Client**
**Project title**
**Scheme report**
**Date**

---

**Table of contents**

### 1 Introduction

1.1 In accordance with your instructions of the [*insert date*] I submit for your consideration my scheme design for [*insert name of project*].

1.2 The feasibility report of the [*insert date*] was approved [*add* with modifications *if appropriate*] on the [*insert date*].

1.3 The outline proposal report of the [*insert date*] was approved [*add* with modifications detailed below *if appropriate*] on the [*insert date*].

1.4 **Summary**

### 2 Terms of reference [*include items as appropriate*]

2.1 The brief is set out in general terms in the feasibility report and modifications, schedule of accommodation and room areas noted in the outline proposal report.
   [*Add the following if appropriate*] I confirm your further instructions modifying and amplifying the brief as follows:
   [*insert full details of modifications with dates received*].

2.2 Further modification of the brief after this stage may incur additional fees and will cause delay.

2.3 A full measured survey of the site/existing property [*omit as appropriate*] has been carried out and is the subject of a separate report.

2.4  A structural analysis has been carried out which indicates [*state the situation*].

2.5  Soil investigations have been carried out and indicate [*state the situation*].

2.6  The following consultants and authorities have been involved in the preparation of this report:
*2.6.1 Consultants*
Quantity surveyors: [*name*]
Structural engineer: [*name*]
Geotechnical engineer: [*name*]
Electrical engineer: [*name*]
Heating and ventilation engineer: [*name*]
Mechanical engineer: [*name*]
Acoustics: [*name*]
Landscape architect: [*name*]
Others: [*name*]
*2.6.2 Authorities*
Planning: [*name*]
Highways: [*name*]
Drainage: [*name*]
Housing: [*name*]
Education: [*name*]
Fire brigade: [*name*]
Transport: [*name*]
British Coal: [*area*]
Electricity: [*area*]
Nuclear Electric: [*area*]
National Power: [*area*]
Powergen: [*area*]
Water: [*area*]
Gas: [*area*]
British Telecom: [*area*]
Police: [*area*]
Forestry Commission: [*area*]
National Trust: [*area*]
Royal Fine Arts Commission
English Heritage.

2.7  The information given is, to the best of my knowledge, correct.

**3  Scheme design** [*include items as appropriate*]

3.1  The detailed proposals are indicated on the drawings.

3.2   The factors affecting the scheme are set out in the feasibility report item 4.

[*If appropriate, add the following*] Further items have become apparent as follows:

[*indicate any further items*].

3.3   **Final scheme analysis** [*more detailed explanation than in the outline proposal report*]

Design philosophy [*general arrangement, relationship of spaces, relationship to surrounding environment, heights, widths, detailed appearance*]

Siting [*considerations, topography, views, orientation, flooding, noise, other pollution, visibility, other*]

Access [*off-road, rail, canal, other*]

Structure [*reinforced concrete, pre- or post-stressed concrete, steel frame, timber frame, space frame, loadbearing brick or block, suspension, other*]

Materials [*roof, walls, internal finishes, external finishes, in detail*]

Heating [*solid fuel, electricity, gas, solar, other – warm air, radiator, underfloor, ceiling panel, other*]

Lighting [*tungsten, fluorescent, flood, spot, other*]

Special treatments [*acoustic, thermal, sound, fire, other*]

Special installations [*lift, ventilation, kitchen, laboratory, fire prevention, provision for disabled, other*]

Special constraints [*particular features for which provision has to be made – statutory undertakings, special equipment, planning requirements, rights, other*]

Other special considerations [*garaging, parking, site area, ministry criteria*].

4   **Phasing** [*include items as appropriate*]

4.1   In accordance with your instructions, the scheme has been prepared on the basis that the project will be carried out in one operation.

4.2   In accordance with your instructions, the project has been designed to be carried out in [*insert number*] phases because [*indicate the reasons – cost, client's operations, planning requirements, other*]. The stages are indicated on the block plan by numbers in bold type:

Stage 1 [*described*]

Stage 2 [*described*] etc.

The results of phasing were indicated in the outline proposal in report item 4.2.

**5**   **Estimate of cost** [*prepared in co-operation with other members of the design team; include items as appropriate*]

5.1   [*Relation to phasing, if any, in 4 above*]

5.2   The following assumptions have been made:
[*indicate any assumptions not clear from the scheme design drawings and general report*].

5.3   The following items have been excluded from the estimate:
[*list excluded items*].

5.4   The figures given below are the best available cost estimate at this stage. The estimate is based upon rates and prices current at the date of this report. No allowance has been made for inflation and the estimate is exclusive of value-added tax (VAT).

5.5   All previous estimates are superseded.

5.6   Estimate [*prepared in co-operation with other members of the design team*]

| | |
|---|---|
| Building contract | £ |
| Additional works [*investigations, supplementary contracts etc.*] | £ |
| Direct works [*furniture, works of art etc.*] | £ |
| Fees and expenses | |
|   Architect | £ |
|   Quantity surveyor | £ |
|   Other consultants | £ |
| Additional items (clerk of works etc.) | £ |
| TOTAL | £ |

5.7   **Total allocated to phases**

| | |
|---|---|
| Stage 1 | £ |
| Stage 2 | £ |
| TOTAL | £ |

[*An alternative would be to split the items in 5.1 according to phasing*]

**6**   **Detailed programme of work**
The following is based upon the assumption that there is no further amendment to the brief or design, consultants provide information on schedule, no difficulties are encountered at tender stage, the site is available on the [*insert date*] and no delays are experienced during the contract period.
Final detailed design complete: [*date*]
Selection of Contractors for tender list: [*date*]

Completion of production drawings: [*date*]
Tenders invited: [*date*]
Receipt of tenders: [*date*]
Start on site: [*date*]
[*insert phasing if applicable*]
Completion on site: [*date*]
End of defects liability period: [*date*].

**7  Approval**
Your approval is requested to the contents of this report and the scheme design. In order that the programme of work in 6 above can be achieved, approval should be received by [*insert date*].

**Appendices**
A   Schedule of accommodation and room sizes
B   Other schedules [*finishes etc.*]
C   Location plan
D   Site plan [*showing phases if applicable*]
E   Scheme design drawings
F   Photographs of model
G   Perspective drawings

# 4.4   Progress reports to client

During the operations on site, it is normal for the architect to report to the client from time to time. It keeps the client informed. It gives him the opportunity to comment and it may keep him away from site. The frequency of such reports depends on the client, the architect and the project. A monthly report would be suitable in most instances, probably timed to go to the client after a site meeting or regular site inspection.

Do not simply send a copy of the clerk of works' report sheet or minutes of the site meetings. They will contain information the client does not need and omit information he requires.

Every client wishes to know the following:

☐   Will the final figure be at or below the contract sum?
☐   If not, why?
☐   Are there any matters which may increase the cost?
☐   Will the project finish on time?
☐   If not, why?
☐   What can be done to improve matters?

The format layout is designed to give him this information clearly and concisely. Your general comments (item 2.8.5) should sum up the situation in few words and lay the groundwork for further approvals or decisions which may be required (item 2.9).

It is essential to number the reports consecutively so that any item in any report can be found simply by reference to the number. For example, the first report will be numbered 1, the second 2 and so on. The first item in the first report would be 1.1, the first item in the second report would be 2.1. The report format shown assumes that it is the second report, for illustrative purposes.

This type of report is useful as a reminder to architect and client of important items. It is also invaluable as a concise record of the state of events at a particular time.

---

# PROGRESS REPORT TO CLIENT FORMAT (Report No. 2)

---

## Client
## Contract title
## Progress report no.
## Date

---

**2.1  Preliminary information**
   *2.1.1* Contract month/week [*omit as appropriate*].
   *2.1.2* Contract completion date
   *2.1.3* Extended completion date [*if applicable*].

**2.2  Progress**
   *2.2.1* Average number of men on site per day since last report. All trades including site agent/foreman/person-in-charge.
   *2.2.2 Total work carried out*

| | |
|---|---|
| Site clearance | % |
| Foundations | % |
| Other sub-structure | % |
| Superstructure | % |
| Internal finishes | % |
| Services | % |
| Special provisions [*specify*] | % |

Drainage                                          %
Landscaping                                       %

[*The actual separation of work can vary to suit the type of project and the amount of detail required by the client*]

## 2.3   Production information
*2.3.1* Drawings issued since last report – nos [*insert numbers*].
*2.3.2* Architect's instructions issued since last report – nos [*insert numbers*].

## 2.4   Client's instructions received since last report
*2.4.1* [*describe*]
*2.4.2* [*describe*]
etc.

## 2.5   Claims received from contractor since last report
*2.5.1 Loss and/or expense*
  Basis
  Amount claimed [£]
This claim is being investigated and will be the subject of a separate report in due course.
*2.5.2 Extension of time*
  Basis
  Delay notified
This notice is being investigated and will be the subject of a separate report in due course.
*2.5.3 Any other claims*
  Breach of contract [*details*]
  Architect's instructions [*details*]
  Certificates [*details*]
  *Ex-gratia* [*details*]
This/these [*omit as appropriate*] claim[s] is/are being investigated and will be the subject of [a] separate report[s] in due course [*omit as appropriate*].

## 2.6   Claims received from other sources since last report
*2.6.1 Statutory undertakings*
  Basis
  Amount claimed [£]
*2.6.2 Adjoining owners*
  Basis
  Amount claimed [£]
*2.6.3 Employer's licensees*
  Basis
  Amount claimed [£]

This/these [*omit as appropriate*] claim[s] is being/are being/has been/have been [*omit as appropriate*] investigated and will be/are [*omit as appropriate*] the subject of [a] separate report[s] in due course/attached [*omit as appropriate*].

**2.7 Cost statement**

| | |
|---|---|
| Contract sum | £ |
| Add/deduct value of architect's instructions issued to date | £ _____ |
| Add contractor's claims agreed | £ _____ |
| | £ _____ |
| Other adjustment [*note in brief*] | £ |
| Estimated final account | £ _____ |

Quantity surveyor's comments

**2.8 General Progress Summary**
*2.8.1 Standard of workmanship*
Action taken [*if necessary*].
*2.8.2 Standard of materials*
Action taken [*if necessary*].
*2.8.3 Delays*
Action taken [*if necessary*].
*2.8.4 Other important occurrences [landslip, discovery of mineshaft etc.]*
Action taken – see separate report no. [*insert number*].
*2.8.5 General comments on the state of the project*

**2.9 Approvals/decisions required**
*2.9.1 [List approvals or decisions required from client with latest dates to avoid claims]*

**Appendix**
Bar or other chart indicating progress to date.

# 4.5 Special reports to client on particular aspects of the contract

From time to time, you may have to report to the client on a special item which either cannot wait for the usual progress report or you have noted as being the subject of a special report. The subject could be as varied as an unexpected collapse on site, the discovery of unforeseen ground conditions or the possibility of determining the contractor's employment. You may feel that a letter to the client is more appropriate in some instances but, unless the matter is very straightforward, the production of even a short report is usually preferable because it imposes a discipline on the matters to be considered.

Special reports should be numbered with the prefix letter 'S' and, if there are several reports, they can be numbered S1, S2 and so on. Future reference to an item in one of the reports would be, for example, S2.3.1, indicating special report 2, section 3, sub-section 1.

# SPECIAL REPORT FORMAT

## Client
## Project title
## Special report no. [*insert number*] on [*insert subject*]
## Date

**S1.1  Introduction**
[*Brief outline of matters or events leading up to or surrounding the subject. Divide into sub-sections if more than one paragraph*]

**S1.2  Problem/event**
*S1.2.1* Situation immediately prior to occurrence
*S1.2.2* Date [*and time*] of occurrence
*S1.2.3* Names and positions of parties involved
*S1.2.4* Concise description of occurrence
*S1.2.5* Situation immediately after occurrence
*S1.2.6* Situation now, including degree of urgency

**S1.3  Factors to take into account**
*S1.3.1* Estimated delay to contract
*S1.3.2* Estimated cost effect to contract
*S1.3.3* Effect on materials and/or workmanship
*S1.3.4* Effect on relations with contractor/sub-contractor/suppliers/consultants
*S1.3.5* Possible claims by any parties
*S1.3.6* Possible claims by client against other parties
*S1.3.7* Contractual position and suggestion for further contractual or legal advice if appropriate

**S1.4 Conclusions**
*S1.4.1* Alternative courses of action
*S1.4.2* Effect of alternative courses of action on delays, costs, claims, relationships, contractual position

**S1.5 Recommendations**
*S1.5.1* Suggested course of action
*S1.5.2* Request for approval to S1.5.1 above or alternative instructions from client
*S1.5.3* Latest date for approval/instructions

**Appendices**
A   Site plan
B   Other relevant drawings

# 4.6   Report to client on contractor's claim for loss and/or expense

There are three types of claim:

❑ Contractual: a claim made under the express provisions of the contract;
❑ Common law: a claim which is based on a breach of contract; and
❑ *Ex-gratia:* a claim made without legal foundation and which the employer is under no obligation to settle. It is sometimes called a hardship claim.

The only type of claim which you are empowered to consider is a claim made under the express provisions of the contract and in accordance with the procedures laid down therein. If the contractor makes a claim at common law or an *ex-gratia* claim, your duty is to notify your clients immediately. Only they can decide such claims. Common law claims are often made as alternatives to contractual claims or because the contractor finds it impossible to comply with one of the contractual stipulations – for example, that the claim must be made within a specific time period. It rarely makes sense for the employer simply to ignore the common law claim, because the chances are that the contractor will pursue it in arbitration. Normally, it is as easy for you to deal with a common law as with a contractual claim and the principle of calculation of damages for breach of contract is identical to the ascertainment of direct loss and/or expense. Before you can deal with such claims, however, you need the consent of the contractor and the authority of the employer. You should notify the employer and seek his authority if you wish to deal with the matter yourself. The following format has been designed to incorporate such notification and request for authority because it forms a useful record.

Although it is your duty to decide the merits of a contractual claim and your [*or the quantity surveyor's*] duty to ascertain the amount of money involved it is advisable to keep your client informed immediately you have made your decision. He will be understandably upset if his first intimation of increased costs is a sum of money in the quantity surveyor's cost statement labelled simply – 'contractor's claim'.

It is suggested that you number your reports with the prefix letter 'S' and file them along with the special reports mentioned in the last section.

---

# REPORT ON CLAIM FOR LOSS AND/ OR EXPENSE FORMAT

---

**Client**
**Project title**
**Special report no.** [*insert number*] **on** [*insert subject*]
**Date**

---

**S2.1   Contract details**
*S2.1.1* Contract sum
*S2.1.2* Contract date for possession
*S2.1.3* Contract date for completion
*S2.1.4* A previous application was made on [*insert date*] in respect of [*insert brief description of claim*]. After consideration, the amount certified was [*insert amount or nil*].

**S2.2   Contractor's claim** [*include items as appropriate*]
*S2.2.1* Date of application
*S2.2.2* Amount claimed [£]
*S2.2.3* Basis of claim
  *[Contractual, common law or ex-gratia.*
    *If contractual, refer to contract clause numbers and alongside each briefly describe the contractor's claim and the amounts claimed under each clause.*

*If common law or ex-gratia, briefly describe the contractor's claim]*

**S2.3 Comments on claim** [*include items as appropriate*]
*S2.3.1* Submitted too early/too late/at the correct time [*omit as appropriate – contractual claims only*]
*S2.3.2* Basis of claim
[*Refer to contract clause numbers and alongside each note whether the claim is agreed in full or reduced, state amounts – contractual claims only*]
*S2.3.3* This application comes into the category of common law/*ex-gratia* [*omit as appropriate*] claim. The architect is not empowered to deal with such claims under the terms of the contract. The contractor's original correspondence is enclosed with this report for your attention. [*Add the following as appropriate*] Taking into account the basis of the common law claim, the amount and the alternative method of dealing with it, it is recommended that it is dealt with in the same way as if it were capable of consideration as a contractual claim. The contractor is happy with this suggestion which will not, of course, prevent him from pursuing the matter at common law later, if he is dissatisfied. Your authority is requested to enable the architect to proceed to deal with the claim in this way.

**S2.4 Factors** [*not applicable to common law or ex-gratia claims*]
*S2.4.1* Relevant events under clause 26.3 of the contract (JCT 80) taken into account [*if other contract amend clause no. as appropriate*]
*S2.4.2* Other factors taken into account

**S2.5 Conclusion** [*not applicable to common law or ex-gratia claims*]
*S2.5.1* Amount ascertained in total [£]
*S2.5.2* The estimated final account will be [£]

**Appendix**
List of all the information supplied by the contractor.

# 4.7 Report to client on grant of extension of time

The clients will receive a copy of the extension of time you make to the contractor but they will appreciate a report from you. Your comments should not be too detailed because it is essentially your own fair and reasonable estimate.

The report should have a prefix 'S' so as to facilitate filing together with reports under the last two sections. For illustrative purposes, the format has been numbered as though it were special report series 3.

---

# REPORT ON GRANT OF EXTENSION OF TIME FORMAT

---

## Client
## Project title
## Special report no. [*insert number*] on [*insert subject*]
## Date

---

**S3.1  Contract details**
*S3.1.1* Contract date for possession
*S3.1.2* Contract date for completion
*S3.1.3* First extension of time made for (... weeks made on [*insert date*])
*S3.1.4* Second extension etc.

**S3.2  Contractor's notice**
*S3.2.1* Date submitted in proper form
*S3.2.2* Basis of notice
[*Refer to contract clause numbers and alongside each briefly describe the contractor's grounds for extension and periods of delay stated under each clause*]

**S3.3  Comments on notice**
*S3.3.1* Submitted too early/too late/at the correct time [*omit as appropriate*]
*S3.3.2* Basis of extension
[*Refer to contract clause numbers and alongside each note the amount of extension (if any) you make*]

**S3.4  Factors**
*S3.4.1* [*Note any special factors you have taken into account*]

**S3.5 Conclusion**
*S3.5.1* Number of weeks/days in the extension
*S3.5.2* New completion date

**Appendix**
List all the information submitted by the contractor with copies if appropriate.

# 5 Miscellaneous Reports

## 5.1 Development possibilities

Whatever may be your own view, the fact is that a sizeable proportion of architectural commissions begin life as speculative ventures. A prospective client may approach you with a site on terms that, if you can show development potential and obtain the necessary permissions, you will have the architectural work involved. Increasingly in recent years, it has been the architect who has made the approach to a prospective client. In such cases, the client is invariably looking for development which will give the best possible return on his investment. Other types of client, such as local authorities or amenity societies may be looking at possible new uses for listed property and they may enlist your help. In this case, a viable use, rather than a profitable investment, is likely to be the key factor. There are countless variations on the theme, such as the partnership situation between local authority and investor to develop run down city centre sites which, nevertheless, contain some buildings of quality.

It is important to remember that the terms on which you agree to take the commission have no bearing on your responsibility to produce a competent report. Paid or unpaid, you will be liable if you overlook something or give negligent advice on which your client acts. Assessment of development potential is a difficult field and you must be careful not to exceed your own area of expertise. In general, you should always make clear that it is for your client to make his own decision about viability based on the information and architectural opinion you provide.

If your clients know what kind of development they want – offices, residential or leisure, for example – the report will follow the normal feasibility report format indicated in Section 4.1. If, however, they wish you to present alternatives for their consideration, the following format will be found useful. Your function is to state facts and put forward suggestions with appropriate cost comparisons. It is probable that you will have to prepare the report very quickly if your client is considering a speculative venture.

# DEVELOPMENT POSSIBILITY REPORT FORMAT

**Client**
**Title** [*address of building or plot of land*]
**Development possibilities**
**Date**

**Table of contents**

**1 Introduction**

1.1 In accordance with your instructions of the [*insert date*] I submit for your consideration my report on the development possibilities of the above site/property [*omit as appropriate*].

1.2 **Summary**

**2 Terms of reference** [*include items as appropriate*]

2.1 It will be appreciated that the report has been prepared within a very short period of time. The contents, however, should enable you to make the basic decision to proceed in a particular development direction. A fully comprehensive report can be prepared later, if required, after a closer investigation of every relevant factor has been carried out.

2.2 A full measured survey of the site/existing property [*omit as appropriate*] has not been carried out at this stage.

2.3 A structural analysis has not been carried out. Therefore, certain assumptions have had to be made pending further investigation.

2.4 The precise site boundaries have yet to be established.

2.5 No soil investigation has been carried out and the report is based on the assumption that ground-bearing and water conditions will prove suitable for building purposes without excessive cost.

2.6 Sketch plans indicate possibilities in the broadest terms.

2.7 The following consultants and authorities have been involved in the preparation of this report:

*2.7.1 Consultants*
Quantity surveyor: [*name*]
Structural engineer: [*name*]
Geotechnical engineer: [*name*]
Electrical engineer: [*name*]
Heating and ventilation engineer: [*name*]
Mechanical engineer: [*name*]
Acoustics: [*name*]
Landscape architect: [*name*]
Others: [*name*]

*2.7.2 Authorities*
Planning: [*name*]
Highways: [*name*]
Drainage: [*name*]
Housing: [*name*]
Education: [*name*]
Fire brigade: [*name*]
Transport: [*name*]
British Coal: [*area*]
Electricity: [*area*]
Nuclear Electric: [*area*]
National Power: [*area*]
Powergen: [*area*]
Water: [*area*]
Gas: [*area*]
British Telecom: [*area*]
Police: [*area*]
Forestry Commission: [*area*]
National Trust: [*area*]
Royal Fine Arts Commission
English Heritage.

2.8 At the time of preparation of this report it had not proved possible to consult the following:
[*list*]
Information given is, to the best of my knowledge, correct. However, it will be appreciated that until formal procedures are concluded (e.g. planning application and negotiation with other authorities) certain parts of this report must be considered as the best information available at the present time as a result of personal interviews with the appropriate officials.

**3  Demand** [*include items as appropriate*]

3.1  **Viability**

   *3.1.1* In order to achieve a viable development of the land/ property [*omit as appropriate*], it is essential, as a first step, to establish that there is a requirement for the type of accommodation proposed.

   *3.1.2* In virtually every area there is a demand for some types of accommodation. There may be a demand in a number of categories.

   *3.1.3* The level of demand must be identified and compared to what it is possible to provide on the site/within the property [*omit phrase as appropriate*].

   *3.1.4* An assessment must be made between the demand in various categories and the development possibilities.

   *3.1.5* In carrying out the assessment, it must be borne in mind that the demand may not be obvious until the general provision in the area has been determined.

3.2  **Shortages**

At first sight, the demand in this area to which appropriate development may be equated is as follows: [*include from the following list, together with other demand, as appropriate*]

Residential [*type*]
Hostels
Hotels
Office [*size*]
Shops [*size*]
Factory units [*size*]
Warehouses [*size*]
Sports centre
Swimming
Outdoor – tennis, golf etc.
Club
Licensed premises
Theatre
Cinema
Exhibition space
Dance hall
Restaurant
School [*type*]
Nursery
Hospital
Clinic
Surgeries

Laboratories
Places of worship.

3.3 **Future trends**
Taking each of the categories separately:
*3.3.1 [insert name of each category in turn]*
Likelihood of future demand can be assessed by:
Existing provision [*describe*]
Viability of existing provision [*describe*]
Known plans for future provision [*describe*].
*3.3.2* The following will affect demand across all categories:
Statistics
Waiting lists
Level of employment
Type of population [*e.g. manual workers, white collar workers, self-employed, number of working wives, number of children in various age groups, number of population of working age, number of population of retirement age*]
Proximity of universities, polytechnics and colleges of further education
Student population over 18 years of age
Observed behaviour patterns.

4 **General site information** [*include items as appropriate*]

4.1 **Site location**
[*Describe the location of the site or property to:*
❑ *Distance from nearest urban centre*
❑ *Topography of the land including notes on existing walls, fences, hedges, trees and buildings*
❑ *Nearby rivers, streams or watercourses, danger of flooding*
❑ *Ownership and use of adjoining land or property*
❑ *Possible nuisances (e.g. factories, airports, motorways)*
❑ *Orientation*]

4.2 **Access**
*4.2.1 Bus services*
The following principal bus services are available from [*insert place and distance*] away [*list*].
*4.2.2 Train services*
The following principal train services are available from [*insert place and distance*] away [*list*].
*4.2.3 Air services*
The following air services are available from [*insert place and distance*] away [*list*].

*4.2.4 Private motorist*

The site lies within [*insert number*] miles of the M [*insert number*] motorway exit [*insert exit number*].

Other readily accessible centres are:

[*name of town or city*] – [*insert number*] miles away.

### 4.3 **Shopping**

Daily shopping needs are well provided for by a number of small shops strategically located.

Mobile shops call at regular intervals.

There are few shops within a 1 mile radius.

The nearest large shopping centre is [*insert number*] miles away at [*insert place*].

There is an open market at [*insert place*] on [*insert days*].

### 4.4 **Health**

Provision for community health is as follows:

Doctors' surgeries [*insert places*]

Dental surgeries [*insert places*]

Opticians [*insert places*]

Chiropodists [*insert places*]

Clinic at [*insert place*]

Health Centre at [*insert place*]

Comprehensive hospital facilities are provided at [*place and distance*] away

Further provision of [*describe provision*] within the next [*insert number*] years is expected at [*insert places*].

### 4.5 **Social and recreational**

Facilities are available as follows:

Public houses: [*insert place and distance*]

Hotels: [*insert place and distance*]

WMC: [*insert place and distance*]

Swimming baths: [*insert place and distance*]

Leisure centre: [*insert place and distance*]

Cricket club: [*insert place and distance*]

Football club: [*insert place and distance*]

Rugby club: [*insert place and distance*]

Angling club: [*insert place and distance*]

Sailing club: [*insert place and distance*]

Community centre: [*insert place and distance*]

Library: [*insert place and distance*]

Art gallery: [*insert place and distance*]

Museum: [*insert place and distance*]

Places of worship:

Anglican: [*insert place and distance*]

Roman Catholic: [*insert place and distance*]
Methodist: [*insert place and distance*]
Baptist: [*insert place and distance*]
Others: [*insert place and distance*]
[*Include any other clubs or social centres nearby*]

## 4.6 Education

The following schools are available:
[*insert place, distance, state, private, mixed or single-sex for each school*]
Nursery/play groups
5–9 years old
9–13 years old
13–16 years old
Sixth form college
Further education.
Further provision of [*describe*] within the next [*insert number*] years is expected at [*insert places*].

## 4.7 Employment

The major employers in the area are:
[*list employers, nature of business, place and distance from site*]
In addition, there is a wide range of minor employers:
[*describe*]
There are, at present, no major employers in the area.

## 5 Factors affecting development [*include items as appropriate*]

## 5.1 Rights

Of light: [*describe*]
Of way: [*describe*]
Of support: [*describe*]
Party walls: [*describe*]
Easements: [*describe*]
Covenants: [*describe*]
Other: [*describe*].

## 5.2 Planning constraints

*5.2.1* The planning authority has raised no objection to the development in principle.

*5.2.2* A previous expired/unexpired [*omit as appropriate*] planning permission was granted for [*describe*].

*5.2.3* The following conditions are expected to be applied to any future approval:

*[list standard conditions and any conditions the planning authority has led you to believe will be imposed on this project].*

5.2.4 The following planning requirements are applicable to this project:

Storey heights: [*specify*]

Number of storeys: [*specify*]

Densities: [*specify*]

Materials: [*specify*]

Access: [*specify*]

Other: [*specify*].

5.2.5 Planning permission has been given for [*describe the nature of the development*] on a piece of land/for buildings [*omit phrase as appropriate and describe the relationship to the site*].

5.2.6 Provisional building lines have been orally agreed as follows:

[*Road or street name*] – [*distance in metres*].

5.2.7 An improvement line will be required to [*insert name of road or street*] as shown on the site plan in the Appendices.

5.2.8 [*Include any other road diversion or closure or planning proposal which may have an effect on the site*]

5.2.9 Full planning approval will be required in due course.

5.2.10 It is thought that planning approval will not be required.

5.2.11 The scheme must comply with the Building Regulations and the appropriate notices must be submitted in due course.

### 5.3  Licensing approvals

Approval will be required from the licensing justices.

### 5.4  Drainage

It is not anticipated that there will be any problems in draining the site; [*or*]

It is anticipated that there may be problems in draining the site [*describe the problems*]. Resolution of the problems could be achieved by [*describe possible solutions*].

### 5.5  Architectural/historical considerations

The site/building [*omit as appropriate*] is situated in a designated conservation area and special care will be required at design stage to obtain planning approval.

The building is listed grade [*insert grade*] and special care will be required at design stage to obtain planning approval.

The existing building is in a conservation area/listed grade [*insert grade or omit as appropriate*] and approval will be required for demolition. Preliminary discussions with the planning authority suggest that such approval will/will not [*omit as appropriate*] be given.

The existing building is not listed but it has some interesting aspects which should be retained if possible:

[*list*]

The proposals for development may be considered sensitive and opposed by local amenity societies.

Consideration should be given to the best way of dealing with possible objections to avoid a public inquiry.

### 5.6   Geological considerations

Available geological information suggests that no unusual precautions will have to be taken at foundation level.

Available geological information suggests that special precautions will have to be taken at foundation level.

A fault/series of faults [*omit as appropriate*] run[s] across the site which will impose constraints upon the layout of the project.

The mining position is [*describe*]. It is considered that all ground settlement has ceased/ground lowering will take place [*omit as appropriate*] but, provided adequate precautions are taken, the project can proceed.

### 5.7   Statutory undertakings and other services

All normal services are available to the site; [*or*]

All normal services are available to the site except [*specify*]. There may be difficulty in overcoming this problem/there should be no insurmountable difficulty in overcoming the problem [*omit as appropriate*].

Diversion of [*specify service or main*] will be required which could prove expensive.

Easements will require to be negotiated for the [*specify*] service.

The electricity supplier will require a sub-station within the site boundary.

The standard procedure for providing street lighting is [*indicate local street lighting procedure*].

[*Add any other information which might affect the project such as high voltage cables over or under the site, government pipelines, complex existing installations etc.*]

### 5.8   Local authority policy

[*State whether the development of the site or property is in accordance with local authority policy, against it, or not applicable. Give brief details and refer to statistics in Appendices.]*

5.9 **Central government policy**
*[As for 5.8 but refer to central government.]*

5.10 **Grant aid**
It is expected that some/substantial [*omit as appropriate*] grant aid may be obtainable from some or all of the following sources:
 *[list appropriate sources]*
It is not expected that any grant aid will be available for development.

5.11 **Structural analysis**
The existing structure appears to be adequate for the purpose of realising a wide variety of development; [*or*]
 The existing structure appears to be inadequate for the purpose of realising any development without further strengthening/replacement [*omit as appropriate*].
 The existing structure would require strengthening for some types of development.
 Special constructional techniques may have to be adopted to avoid damage to neighbouring property.

5.12 **Site access**
Access to the site is possible at the following points:
 *[describe with any comments necessary]*.

6 **Principal development possibilities**
*[Examine each category in relation to the site or property and study under the following heads]*

6.1 **Planning options**

6.2 **Structural options**

6.3 **Design options**

6.4 **Heating and fuel options**

6.5 **Other specially applicable options**

7 **Phasing possibilities** *[include items as appropriate]*

7.1 The possibilities for phased development vary considerably depending upon the category of development under consideration.

7.2 **Categories**
[*Under each category, the possible phasing should be set out*]
Stage 1 [*describe*]
Stage 2 [*describe*]

8 **Estimate of cost** [*prepared in co-operation with other members of the design team, include items as appropriate*]

8.1 The financial return on capital investment is something to be assessed by you or your financial advisors. I can provide approximate estimates of total construction and associated costs for each category of development.

8.2 Categories [*Under each category, the best available estimates should be set out in the following way, showing relation to phasing if appropriate*]

| | |
|---|---|
| Building contract | £ |
| Additional works [*investigations,* | |
| *supplementary contracts etc.*] | £ |
| Assumed direct works [*furniture,* | |
| *works of art etc.*] | £ |
| Fees and expenses | |
| Architect | £ |
| Quantity surveyor | £ |
| Other consultants | £ |
| Additional items (clerk of works etc.) | £ |
| TOTAL | £ |

8.3 No attempt, at this stage, has been made to assess maintenance and running costs in each category.

8.4 It must be appreciated that the cost figures can only be considered to be approximate until a detailed scheme design has been carried out on a particular category.

8.5 The estimate is based upon rates and prices current at the date of this report. No allowance has been made for inflation and the estimate is exclusive of value-added tax (VAT).

9 **Programme of work** [*include items as appropriate*]

9.1 On the assumption that firm decisions, approvals and instructions to proceed are given by [*insert date*], the work of the design team and contract periods are expected to be:
[*category*] – [*design team period*] – [*contract period unphased*] – [*contract period phased*]
[*Repeat for each category*]

9.2   It is not practicable at this stage to give a reasonable indication of the periods of time to be allocated to the design team or the construction work. I will be pleased to supply this information on receipt of your further instructions.

### 10   Conclusions

10.1   [*Assessment of options in brief and suggested best option, from demand/construction point of view – not based on cost*]

10.2   Your instructions are requested to proceed with the preparation of outline proposals for one of the categories of development in 10.1 above.

### Appendices
A   Location plan
B   Site plan
C   Aerial and other photographs
D   Copy of geological report and plans [*if available*]
E   Copy of mining report [*if appropriate*]
F   Bibliography
G   Diagrammatic proposals [*if appropriate*]

## 5.2   Inspection of property

### 5.2.1   Purpose

A generally phrased request from your client for an inspection of property may cover inspections for a number of purposes. It is logical to consider them separately. Thus, inspections before purchase or before work commences would fall under this section; inspections for the purpose of determining condition (e.g. before underpinning or before leasing would fall under Section 5.3; particular inspections to discover the cause and suggest remedies for defects are covered by Section 5.4).

The various types of inspection have aspects in common. They will be considered in some detail here and the reader will be referred back to this section when other types of inspection are considered. This section will deal with the inspections required before purchase or before construction work commences.

### 5.2.2   Preparations

Make absolutely sure of the address of the property and obtain all necessary keys. It is not unknown for an architect or surveyor to make an inspection of the wrong property, particularly if a number of properties are standing together empty. It is even more common, and intensely irritating, to arrive on site and find that some parts of the property are inaccessible because of lack of keys.

Obtain a site plan of the property and get your client or his solicitor to mark the boundaries and his ownership clearly.

It is particularly useful if you can obtain existing plans of the building. Although they must be treated with caution, they often show unsuspected relationships of rooms, later additions can be deduced and concealed details such as columns, beams and even rainwater pipes may be shown. Sources for drawings are the client himself, local authority deposited plans and local archives, where even old maps of the area can yield useful information about the age of the property. Do not overlook the Deeds Registry or County Office as a source of information.

Make absolutely sure that you have got all the appropriate equipment with you (see Appendix A).

## 5.2.3   Procedure

The first thing to do after arriving at the site is to walk around the boundary and observe the general surroundings, condition of fences, boundary walls and hedges. Have a look at the buildings externally, paying particular attention to the roof and fall pipes. Then go inside and look around in each room. This part of the inspection, although essentially preliminary, should never be skimped. By this time, you should have got the 'feel' of the property. Is it:

❑ Neglected but basically sound structurally?
❑ In good repair?
❑ In poor condition structurally, perhaps with some ominous cracks and bulges?

The next stage is to work through the property systematically, measuring and making notes. It is a good idea to prepare a rough plan of each floor of the building and sketches of each elevation before you begin. Inevitably you will have to supplement your sketches as you go along, probably with sections through awkward places.

Start on the top floor of the building and deal with each room from left to right, leaving the corridor or landing on each floor to the last. Inside each room deal with each wall, again left to right, then ceiling and floor. Ideally you should examine the roof void first but some people prefer to leave it to the end to avoid trailing dirt through the building, particularly if it is still furnished. If the building is very large with numerous staircases and completely separate parts, you should still observe the left to right system in whatever area you are working. There are two basic methods of logging the results:

❑ Consider all like things together (e.g. windows, doors, floors, ceilings etc.); or
❑ Deal with each item within the room as you come to it.

There are arguments for each method but the author prefers the second method because it lessens the chance of omissions.

After completing the interior, carefully note the external features, taking each elevation in turn and working from roof to ground level and from left to right. When you have completed the building, including any outbuildings, walk around the boundaries of the property noting the condition. Pick up any other noteworthy features such as trees, wells and flagged paths. Finally check the manholes and plot all drain runs, internal and external.

Often, you will be required to survey the whole building so that you can prepare proper measured drawings. It is usually best to do this first, after you have made a preliminary inspection and before you start taking detailed notes of condition. The exception to this is if, on your preliminary inspection, you discover some really serious fault which may make the whole survey abortive. In such a case, you will clearly wish to report immediately to your client, probably by telephone to obtain further instructions. Always confirm such further instructions in writing.

The various points, together with additional information which may be of interest, must be carefully gathered together and presented in such a way that your client can readily appreciate the implications. This can be done in various ways.

The best kind of report is thorough and detailed. The following report format is based on that principle. Note that, although you will have carried out your internal survey starting at the top of the building and working down for practical reasons, the format indicates the reverse order for presentation of the report. Experience suggests that your client will more readily appreciate this approach.

It may be, however, that your client requires little detail in the final report although you will be involved in considerable detailed work to produce it. In such cases the format can be used as a checklist and the final report will be composed of only items 1, 2, 3, 4, 9 and 10.

The so-called 'visual report' is an ill-defined concept. If you are asked to prepare a visual report of property, your client probably means that he wants you to spend as little time as is consistent with obtaining the information he requires. It is important, therefore, to be sure just why the client wants the report and a note regarding the purpose to which the report can be put should be inserted in the terms of reference, but see Chapter 11. How much detail you eventually include will depend on your client's purpose. A short report, as indicated above, may well suffice in most cases, but you should work through the format/checklist for your own records. Reports for valuation purposes must only be attempted if you have the necessary expertise.

# INSPECTION OF PROPERTY REPORT FORMAT

**Client**
**Address of property**
**Purpose of report**
**Date of inspection**
**Date of report**

**Table of contents**

**1 Introduction**

1.1 In accordance with your instructions of the [*insert date*], I submit for your consideration my inspection report on the above property.

1.2 **Summary**

**2 Terms of reference** [*include items as appropriate*]

2.1 This report embraces the inspection only of the property.

2.2 The report has been prepared on the understanding that it is only to be used for [*specify*].

2.3 A separate measured survey has been carried out. Details are included as an Appendix.

2.4 It has not been possible to inspect [*describe the places not inspected*] in the time available/without special equipment [*omit one or both phrases as appropriate*].

2.5  The following parts of the property have not been inspected: [*list*].

**3  General information** [*include items as appropriate*]

3.1  **Site location**
[*Describe the location of the site or property to:*
- *Distance from nearest urban centre*
- *Ownerships and uses of adjoining land or property*
- *Nearby rivers, streams or watercourses, danger of flooding*
- *Possible nuisances (e.g. factories, airports, motorways)*
- *Orientation*].

3.2  **Access**
*3.2.1  Bus services*
The following principal bus services are available from [*place and distance*] away:
[*list main services and regularity*].
*3.2.2  Train services*
The following principal train services are available from [*place and distance*] away:
[*list main services and regularity*].
*3.2.3  Air services*
The following air services are available from [*place and distance*] away:
[*list main services and regularity*].
*3.2.4  Private motorist*
The site lies within [*insert number*] miles of the M [*insert number*] motorway exit [*insert number*].
   Other readily accessible centres are:
[*Name of town or city*] – [*insert number*] miles.

3.3  **Shopping**
Daily shopping needs are well provided for by a number of small shops strategically located.
Mobile shops call at regular intervals.
There are few shops within 1 mile radius.
The nearest large shopping centre is [*insert number*] miles away at [*insert place*].
There is an open market at [*insert place*] on [*insert days*].

3.4  **Health**
Provision for community health is as follows:
   Doctors' surgeries [*insert places*]
   Dental surgeries [*insert places*]
   Opticians [*insert places*]

Chiropodists [*insert places*]
Clinic at [*insert place*]
Health Centre at [*insert place*]
Comprehensive hospital facilities are provided at [*place and distance*] away
Further provision of [*describe provision*] within the next [*insert number*] years is expected at [*insert places*].

3.5 **Social and recreational**
Facilities are available as follows:
Public houses: [*insert place and distance*]
Hotels: [*insert place and distance*]
WMC: [*insert place and distance*]
Swimming baths: [*insert place and distance*]
Leisure centre: [*insert place and distance*]
Cricket club: [*insert place and distance*]
Football club: [*insert place and distance*]
Rugby club: [*insert place and distance*]
Angling club: [*insert place and distance*]
Sailing club: [*insert place and distance*]
Community centre: [*insert place and distance*]
Library: [*insert place and distance*]
Art gallery: [insert place and distance]
Museum: [*insert place and distance*]
Places of worship:
Anglican: [*insert place and distance*]
Roman Catholic: [*insert place and distance*]
Methodist: [*Insert place and distance*]
Baptist: [*insert place and distance*]
Others: [*insert place and distance*]
[*Include any other clubs or social centres nearby*]

3.6 **Education**
The following schools are available:
[*insert place, distance, state, private, mixed or single-sex for each school*]
Nursery/play groups
5–9 years old
9–13 years old
13–16 years old
Sixth form college
Further education
Further provision of [*describe*] within the next [*insert number*] years is expected at [*insert places*].

3.7 **Employment**
The major employers in the area are:
[*list employers, nature of business, place and distance from site*]
In addition, there is a wide range of minor employers:
[*describe*]
There are, at present, no major employers in the area.

   **4 Special factors** [*include items as appropriate*]

4.1 **Rights**
Of light: [*describe*]
Of way: [*describe*]
Of support: *describe*]
Party walls: [*describe*]
Easements: [*describe*]
Covenants: [*describe*]
Other: [*describe*]

4.2 **Planning**
*4.2.1* Planning permission was obtained for [*describe*]. It is no longer/still [*omit as appropriate*] applicable.
*4.2.2* [*Describe any planning permissions which have been applied for or obtained in respect of neighbouring land or property*]
*4.2.3* [*Describe any road diversions or improvement lines which may affect the site*]
*4.2.4* The property is situated in a designated conservation area.
*4.2.5* The property is a listed building grade [*insert grade*].
*4.2.6* There is a tree preservation order on [*insert number, and location of trees*].

4.3 **Mining**
[*Describe the situation*].

4.4 **Statutory undertakings**
All normal services are available to the property; [*or*]
All normal services are available to the property except [*specify*].

   **5 Exterior of building** [*include items as appropriate*]

5.1 **Roof**
*5.1.1 Types*
Double-pitched
Mono-pitched

Broken-pitched
Mansard
Flat
Barrel-vault
Domed
Other
*5.1.2 Materials*
Slates [*type*]
Tiles [*type*]
Stone
Shingles
Lead
Copper
Zinc
Aluminium
Asphalt
Bituminous felt [*type*]
Composite
Proprietary plastic [*name*]
Other
Condition
*5.1.3 Chimneys*
Brick
Stone
Cast iron
Plastic
Asbestos
Condition
*5.1.4 Gutters*
Valley
Eaves
Secret
Chimney
Parapet
Slates
Tiles
Lead
Copper
Zinc
Aluminium
Asphalt
Bituminous felt
Composite
Proprietary plastic [*name*]

Asbestos cement
Cast iron
Pressed steel
Sealed timber
Size
Condition
*5.1.5 Rooflights*
Materials
Size
Condition
*5.1.6 Dormers*
Type [*pitched, flat, other*]
Materials
Size
Construction
Condition
*5.1.7 Other projections through roof*
Type
Materials
Size
Condition
*5.1.8 Flashings*
Lead
Copper
Composite
Proprietary plastic [*name*]
Zinc
Aluminium
Bituminous felt
Position
Condition

5.2  **Walls**
*5.2.1 Exposed basement*
Brick [*name and bond*]
Stone [*name and bond*]
Blocks [*type and bond*]
Rendering [*type*] on . . .
Weatherboard [*type, material and finish*]
Cedar shingles
Tile hanging
Concrete panel [*finish*]
Timber panel
Columns [*material and spacing*]
Total thickness

Construction
Condition
*5.2.2 Ground flooor [as above]*
*5.2.3 First floor [as above]*
*5.2.4 Second floor [as above]*
etc.
*5.2.5 Special features*
  Buttresses
  Arches
  Blind arcading
  String courses
  Corbels
  Plinths
  Material
  Condition
*5.2.6 Damp proof course*
  Bituminous felt [*type*]
  Asphalt [*thickness*]
  Lead [*grade and thickness*]
  Copper
  Slate
  Tile [*number of courses*]
  Engineering brick [*number of courses*]
  Plastic [*type*]
  Proprietary [*name*]
  Position
  Condition
*5.2.7 Air bricks*
  Brick
  Cast iron
  Terracotta
  Size
  Regularity
  Condition
*5.2.8 Foundations [if examined]*
  Concrete strip
  Ditto, reinforced
  Concrete pile and beam
  Concrete raft
  Concrete pad
  Brick footings
  None
  Size
  Depth to underside
  Condition

5.3 **Rainwater pipes**
Cast iron
Pressed steel
Lead
Copper
Asbestos cement
Sealed timber
Size
Location
Aluminium
Plastic [*type*]
Condition

5.4 **Windows and cills** [*window type will be noted in the internal listing*]
Timber
Plastic
Plastic-covered timber
Aluminium
Galvanised steel
Finish
Condition

5.5 **Doors**
*5.5.1 Door 1*
Timber
Aluminium
Galvanised steel
Glazing [*size and type*]
Finish
Lock type [*condition*]
Threshold [*material, condition*]
Furniture
Aluminium
Bronze
Cast iron
Galvanised steel
Brass
Chrome on . . .
Plastic
Type [*knob, lever, pull, escutcheon, kicking plate, push plate, letter plate, bolt, butts, knocker, bell, chimes*]
*5.5.2 Door 2* [*as above*]
*5.5.3 Door 3* [*as above*]

**6  Interior of building** [*include items as appropriate*]

6.1  **Basement**
*6.1.1  Room 1* [*taking in order as described in 5.2.3*]

(i) Walls
Exposed brickwork
Exposed stonework
Exposed blockwork
Exposed concrete
Plaster on brick
Plaster on stone
Plaster on block
Plaster on concrete
Plaster on lath or plasterboard on solid
Plaster on lath or plasterboard on studding
Board [*acoustic, timber, other*] on lath or studding
Tiles [*acoustic, plaster, other*] on lath or studding or solid
Rendering
Finish – paper [*type*]
Finish – paint [*type*]
Finish – tiles [*type*]
Condition

(ii) Ceiling
Exposed brick, stone, concrete, timber
Plaster
Plaster on lath or plasterboard
Board [*acoustic, timber, other*]
Tiles [*acoustic, plaster, other*]
Suspension system
Finish – paper [*type*]
Finish – paint [*type*]
Finish – tiles [*type*]
Condition

(iii) Floor
Concrete
Reinforced concrete [*pre-cast or in situ*]
Hardwood joists
Softwood joists
Composite – concrete and steel
Composite – concrete and timber
Composite – steel and timber
Solid or suspended
Thickness
Damp proof membrane [*material and thickness*]
Condition

Finishes
    Hardwood strip, blocks, tiles
    Softwood boards
    Chipboard [*thickness*]
    Asphalt [*thickness*]
    Screed [*type and thickness*]
    Terrazzo
    Quarry tiles
    Brick paviors
    Stone [*flags, setts, sizes*]
    Slate
    Cork tiles
    Rubber sheet, tiles [*type*]
    Plastic sheet, tiles [*type*]
    Linoleum [*thickness*]
    Carpet sheet, tiles
    Polished
    Painted
    Stained
    Sealed
    Varnished
    Condition
[*If this is the lowest floor, note if possible, whether there is site concrete, space under joists, sleeper walls, material, debris*]

(iv) Windows
    Location
    Size
    Timber
    UPVC
    Plastic-covered timber
    Aluminium
    Galvanised steel
    Finish
    Type: fixed; vertical sliding; horizontal sliding; casement; top hung; bottom hung; centre pivot vertical; centre pivot horizontal; louvred; double framed
    Finish condition
    Glass type: float; sheet; cast; plate; armoured; laminated; obscure; bottle; double- or single-glazed; painted; stained
    Glass condition
    Window board; casings; architraves; shutters [*material, finish and condition*]
    Furniture [*material, type and condition*]

(v) Doors
  Size
  Hardwood
  Softwood
  Aluminium
  Galvanised steel
  Rubber
  Panelled
  Flush
  Glazing [*type and position*]
  Finish
    Polished
    Painted
    Stained
    Sealed
    Varnished
  Condition
  Latches [*types*]
  Locks [*types*]
  Furniture
    Aluminium
    Bronze
    Cast iron
    Galvanised steel
    Brass
    Chrome on . . .
    Plastic
    Wood
    Ceramic
    Type: knob; lever; pull; escutcheon; kicking plate; push
      plate; bolt; butts; closer; hooks
  Condition
  Frames, casings, architraves [*materials, types, finish and
    condition*]

(vi) Fireplaces
  Description
  Size
  Location
  Material
  Finish
  Grates [*types*]
  Surround [*materials*]
  Hearth [*materials*]
  Mantelpiece [*materials*]

Flue
Condition

(vii) Built-in furniture
Description
Location
Materials
Finish
Furniture [*type, material*]
Condition

(viii) Skirtings
Type [*plain, chamfered, moulded*]
Size
Hardwood
Softwood
Plastic
Quarry tiles
Rendered
Finish
   Polished
   Painted
   Stained
   Sealed
   Varnished
Condition

(ix) Picture rails and pelmets
Size
Hardwood
Softwood
Plastic
Aluminium
Finish
   Polished
   Painted
   Stained
   Sealed
   Varnished
Condition

(x) Cornice and ceiling rose
Type
Plaster
Timber
Expanded polystyrene
Finish – papered
Finish – painted
Condition

(xi) Ventilation grilles
  Type
  Size
  Location
  Plaster
  Timber
  Metal
  Finish
  Condition

(xii) Hooks etc. [*numbers, location, material, finish, condition*]

(xiii) Partitions [*not full height*]
  Brick
  Stone
  Block
  Metal [*type*]
  Studding
  Plaster on . . .
  Plastic on . . .
  Proprietary
  Height
  Condition

(xiv) Lighting
  Number
  Location
  Type [*tungsten, fluorescent, flood, spot etc.*]
  Materials
  Condition

(xv) Socket outlets
  Number
  Location
  Type [*LV, power, 13 amp, ring circuit*]
  Material
  Condition

(xvi) Heating
  Location
  Type [*radiator, warm air, underfloor, ceiling panel*]
  Materials
  Condition

*6.1.2 Room 2 [as 6.1.1 above]*
*6.1.3 Room 3 [as 6.1.1 above]*
etc.
*6.1.4 Corridors, landings, lobbies, halls [as 6.1.1 above]*
*6.1.5 Staircase [as 6.1.1 above and:]*
  Type [*straight flight, curved, dog-leg, spiral etc.*]
  Location

Stone
Brick
Concrete [*pre-cast or in situ*]
Hardwood
Softwood
Cast iron
Treads and risers [*materials, finishes and condition*]
Strings [*materials, finishes and condition*]
Balusters [*materials, finishes and condition*]
Handrails [*materials, finishes and condition*]
Panelling [*materials, finishes and condition*]
Apron [*materials, finishes and condition*]
Special features [*scrolls, winders, open tread, open stairs, bull-nosed bottom step*]
Condition
Soffit [*materials, finish and condition*]

*6.1.6  Bathrooms and other sanitary units [as 6.1.1 above and:]*

(i) Bath
Number
Type [*low-level, non-slip, hip etc.*]
Vitreous enamel on cast iron
Vitreous enamel on pressed steel
Vitreous china
Perspex
Fibreglass
Size
Colour
Condition
Panel [*material, colour and condition*]
Fittings [*taps, mixers, shower, plugs and chain, handles, materials and condition*]
Waste [*size, trap, material and condition*]

(ii) Shower
Number
Size
Vitreous china
Glazed earthenware
Perspex
Fibreglass
Glazed tiles
Mosaic
Cement render
Colour
Condition

Fittings [*shower type and condition*]
Waste [*size, trap, material and condition*]
Screen or curtain [*materials and condition*]

(iii) Wash basin
Number
Type [*pedestal, on brackets, in vanity unit, corner, etc.*]
Size
Vitreous enamel on cast iron
Vitreous enamel on pressed steel
Vitreous china
Glazed earthenware
Perspex
Fibreglass
Colour
Condition
Fittings [*taps, mixers, plugs and chain, materials and condition*]

(iv) Water closet
Number
Type [*pedestal, cantilever, low-level etc.*]
Size
Vitreous china
Glazed earthenware
Colour
Condition
Flush tank [*materials, position, operation, capacity, colour, condition*]
Seat and cover [*materials, colour and condition*]

(v) Bidet
Number
Type
Size
Vitreous china
Glazed earthenware
Colour
Condition
Fittings [*taps, materials and condition*]
Waste [*size, trap, material and condition*]

(vi) Urinal
Number
Type [*single cantilevered, floor, range*]
Size
Vitreous china
Glazed earthenware

Stainless steel
Glazed tile
Cement render
Colour
Condition
Fittings [*sparge pipes, materials and condition*]
Waste [*size, trap, material and condition*]
Flush tank [*material, position, operation, capacity, colour, condition*]

(vii) Soap tray or dispenser [*number, material, type, colour, size and condition*]

(viii) Towel rail or dispenser [*number, material, type, colour, size and condition*]

(ix) Toilet roll holder [*number, material, type, colour, size and condition*]

(x) Hat and coat hooks [*number, material, type, colour, size and condition*]
*6.1.7 Kitchen [as 6.1.1 above and:]*

(i) Sinks
Number
Type [*single, double drainer etc.*]
Size
Vitreous enamel on cast iron
Vitreous enamel on pressed steel
Vitreous china
Glazed earthenware
Stainless steel
Perspex
Fibreglass
Colour
Method of support
Condition
Fittings [*taps, mixer, materials, plug and chain and condition*]
Waste [*size, trap, material and condition*]

(ii) Work surfaces and shelving
Number
Size
Hardwood
Softwood
Plastic
Colour
Method of support
Condition

(iii) Units [*number, material, type, size, position, condition*]

(iv) Cooking equipment
   Type
   Manufacturer
   Size
   Age
   Position
   Condition

(v) Ventilation
   Location
   Type [*air brick, mechanical, hoods etc.*]
   Condition

(vi) Floor drainage
   Material
   Type [*channel, sloping floor, grid, galley*]
   Condition

(vii) Isolated taps
   Location
   Number
   Size
   Material
   Condition.

6.2 **Ground floor** [*Repeat as for 6.1 above as appropriate*]

6.3 **First floor** [*Repeat as for 6.1 above as appropriate*]
   etc.

6.4 **Roof space** [*if any*]
   *6.4.1 Construction*
      Timber
      Laminated timber
      Steel
      Reinforced concrete
      Sizes and spacing of members
      Insulation material and thickness
      Damp proofing
      Vapour barrier
      Condition
   *6.4.2 Walls*
      Brick
      Stone
      Block [*type*]
      Concrete
      Timber
      Render on...
      Condition

*6.4.3 Party walls*
Brick
Stone
Concrete
Timber
Block [*type*]
Render on ...
Condition
*6.4.4 Chimneys*
Location
Brick
Stone
Block [*type*]
Concrete
Render on ...
Flues, number, gather
Condition
*6.4.5 Roof lights and dormers*
Location
Sizes
Construction
Furniture
Condition
*6.4.6 Lighting*
Location
Type [*tungsten, fluorescent, flood, spot etc.*]
Material
Condition
*6.4.7 Socket outlets*
Location
Type [*LV, power, 13 amp, ring circuit*]
Material
Condition
*6.4.8 Access*
Location
Size
Type [*door, trap*]
Locks and other furniture
Ladder [*material*]
Stair [*material*]
Condition
*6.4.9 Flooring*
Location
Material
Condition

*6.4.10 Service equipment in roof space*

(i) Storage tanks
   Location
   Capacities
   Cold or hot
   Expansion
   Materials
   Leakage reservoir [*material*]
   Feed pipes [*size and material*]
   Overflow pipes [*size and material*]
   Other pipes [*size and material*]
   Ball valves [*size and material*]
   Insulation and lids [*material*]
   Condition

(ii) Heating pipes
   Location
   Sizes
   Materials
   Insulation
   Condition

(iii) Ducting
   Location
   Size
   Material
   Insulation
   Condition

(iv) Electric conduit
   Location
   Sizes
   Material
   Condition

(v) TV aerial
   Location
   Type
   Condition

(vi) Lift installation
   Location
   Overall size
   Manufacturer
   Condition

(vii) Hooks, pulleys, wheels, ventilators etc.
   Location
   Material

Size
Condition.

6.5 **Services**
  *6.5.1 Electricity*
  Intake position [*underground or high level*]
  Single or three phase
  Meter type
  Consumer unit [*type, circuit break provision, loading*]
  Circuits
  Wiring [*conduit, surface, concealed, materials*]
  Age
  Other electrical equipment not included elsewhere [*age and
    condition*]
  *6.5.2 Gas*
  Intake position
  Meter [*type and size*]
  Pipe materials [*copper, galvanised steel, lead, composition*]
  Position, size and type of all gas points
  Age
  Condition
  *6.5.3 Water*
  Intake position
  Size
  Stop tap and drain-off cock positions
  Materials
  Age
  Condition
  *6.5.4 Heating and hot water*
  Fuel [*electricity, gas, oil, solid, solar*]
  Type
    High pressure hot water
    Low pressure hot water
    Pump-assisted or gravity
    Boiler [*size, position, material, manufacturer*]
    Radiators
    Skirting heating
    Fan assisted
    Pipework [*material and sizes*]
    Blown warm air
    Underfloor electric
    Underfloor hot water
    Storage heaters
    Ceiling panel heaters
    Age
    Condition

Cylinder
  Location
  Capacity
  Direct or indirect
  Material
  Insulation
  Condition
Immersion heater [*size and condition*]
Gas heater [*size, location and condition*]
6.5.5 *Telephone*
  Intake position [*underground or high level*]
  Switchboard [*number of lines and location*]
  Position of handsets
  Position of extensions
  Plug-in system
  Age
  Telephone number
6.5.6 *Other services*
  Cable radio [*location and condition*]
  Cable TV [*location and condition*]
  Computer terminals
  Compressed air pipes
  Vacuum pipes
  Television aerial [*location and condition*]
  Television dish [*location and condition*]
  Lightning conductor [*location and condition*]

**7 Outbuildings** [*include items as appropriate*]

7.1 [*Type*]
  Location
  Wall construction and condition
  Roof construction and condition
  Floor construction and condition
  Windows [*materials and condition*]
  Doors [*materials and condition*]
  Damp proof courses [*materials, position and condition*]
  Disposal of rainwater [*materials, position and condition*]
  Services [*water, gas, electricity*]
  Access

7.2 [*Type*] [*as for 7.1 above*]
  etc.

**8 Surroundings within curtilage** [*include items as appropriate*]

8.1 **Paving**
  Entrance drive
  Entrance path

Paving surrounding building
Terrace
Patio
Steps [*number and width*]
Paths generally
Concrete [*in situ, slabs*]
Tarmac
Gravel [*type*]
Brick
Stone
Tiles
Sizes
Condition

8.2 **Boundaries**
Location
Ownership [*if certain*]
Wall
   Thickness
   Height
   Buttresses [*sizes and spacing*]
   Brick
   Stone
   Concrete block [*type*]
   Concrete
   Condition
Fence
   Type
   Height
   Timber
   Concrete
   Plastic
   Condition
Hedge
   Type
   Height and thickness
   Condition
Water
   Sea
   Lake
   Stream
   Canal
   Ditch
   Condition of bank

8.3 **Grounds**
  *8.3.1 General form*
  Flat
  Sloping [*e.g. east to west approx. .... metres overall*]
  Undulating
  *8.3.2 Trees*
  Types
  Number
  Location
  Condition
  *8.3.3 Bushes*
  Types
  Number
  Location
  Condition
  *8.3.4 Cultivation*
  Lawn [*size*]
  Vegetable garden [*size*]
  Flower beds
  Condition
  *8.3.5 Special features*

  (i) Well
  Location
  Size
  Depth
  Construction
  Condition

  (ii) Pond
  Location
  Size
  Depth
  General condition [*including banks*]

  (iii) Underground tanks
  Type
  Location
  Size
  Construction
  Depth
  Condition

  (iv) Swimming pool
  Location
  Size
  Depth
  Construction

Equipment
Condition.

8.4  **Drainage**
Combined or separate

(i) Foul pipes
Salt-glazed stoneware
Pitch fibre
Asbestos cement
Plastic [*manufacturer*]
Size
Type of jointing
Condition

(ii) Inspection chambers
Location
Number
Size
Wall thickness
Brick
Stone
Concrete
Render on . . .
Number of branches and sizes
Interceptor trap
Fresh air inlet
Back drop
Anti-flood trap
Cleaning eye and plug
Cover
Condition

(iii) Discharge to
Public sewer
Septic tank
Cesspool

(iv) Septic tank
Type
Location
Size and number of chambers
Construction
Cover
Discharge to . . .
Condition

(v) Cesspool
Type

Location
Size
Construction
Cover
Condition

(vi) Gulleys
Type
Location
Number
Size
Salt-glazed stoneware
Cast iron
Plastic [*manufacturer*]
Condition

(vii) Surface water
Pipes [*as for foul*]
Inspection chambers [*as for foul*]
Silt pit: location; construction [*brick, concrete, fibre glass*]; size and number of chambers; condition
Discharge to: public sewer; watercourse; soakaway [*type, size, construction, materials*]; condition
Land drainage: location; salt-glazed stoneware [*perforated, open joint*]; pitch fibre; asbestos cement; plastic [*manufacturer*]; condition.

**9 Conclusions** [*include items as appropriate*]

9.1 It is recommended that the following parts of the building should be made available for inspection:
[*list any parts of the building which it was not possible to inspect but which you consider should be inspected*].

9.2 It is recommended that the following consultant[s] should be requested to carry out [an] inspection[s]:
Structural engineer
Electrical engineer
Heating, ventilation and mechanical engineer
Sanitary engineer
Timber rot and infestation specialist
Acoustic engineer
Landscape architect
Fire brigade.

9.3 **General structural condition**
[*Give a description of the general structural condition, including particular reference to any items giving cause for concern even if already noted in the main section of the report*]

9.4   **General condition of finishes**
[*Give a description of the general state of finishes and classify under one of the following heads:*
- ❏   *Excellent – no work required*
- ❏   *Well maintained –little work required*
- ❏   *Fair – some work required*
- ❏   *Poor – a great deal of work required*
- ❏   *Very poor – complete replacement required*]

9.5   **Weathertight condition**
[*Describe areas suffering from ingress of damp including defective damp proof courses, windows and doors*]

9.6   **General remarks**
[*Include any particular problems or features in the building and curtilage as a whole – keep as brief as possible*]

10   **Instructions** [*include items as appropriate*]
Your instructions are requested as follows:
   [*insert appropriate statement[s] from following list*].

10.1   To carry out inspections indicated in 9.1 above.

10.2   To instruct consultants, on your behalf, to carry out inspections indicated in 9.2 above.

10.3   [*Any further instructions you may require*]

**Appendices**
A   Measured drawings [*if required*]
B   Tree survey

# 5.3   Schedule of condition (dilapidation)

## 5.3.1   Terms

There is often confusion regarding the precise meaning and application of terms when inspection of property is being discussed. A client may ask for an 'inspection', 'schedule of condition' or a 'schedule for dilapidation' and mean exactly the same thing. Although the client may be confused, it is important for you, as the professional, to understand the difference.

An 'inspection' is usually carried out before purchase. It has been outlined in Section 5.2 together with a lengthy report format/checklist. It forms the basis of all reports on existing property. The basic difference between a 'schedule of condition' and a 'schedule for dilapidation' is that the former records precise condition and state of repair, whereas the latter records the same information but takes into account the responsibility of tenant and landlord and differentiates between them.

## 5.3.2   Purpose and timing

A schedule of condition is carried out in the following circumstances:

❑   Before carrying out operations in, or in the vicinity of, buildings (e.g. adaptations, piling, underpinning, work to party walls) when it is essential to record the precise condition of structure and finishes; this is so that the effect of the work can be determined with great accuracy after operations have been completed.
❑   Before the commencement of a lease in order to record the state of repair.

A schedule for dilapidation records lack of repair and it may be carried out in the following circumstances:

❑   During the terms of a lease to ensure that the tenant is not neglecting his duty with regard to repairs.
❑   Before termination of a lease (say, two months before) to ensure that all repairs have been done before termination takes place.
❑   Immediately after termination of a lease to check that all repairs, which are the responsibility of the tenant, have been carried out.

## 5.3.3   Procedure

Because of the basic similarities, condition and dilapidation are considered together. The procedure that should be adopted is very much the same as that followed when carrying out an inspection before purchase (see Sections 5.2.2 and 5.2.3). However, certain aspects should be examined more carefully and given more weight in the report. Other items, which would be of great interest to a prospective purchaser, are of no consequence in this particular section. For example, the frequency of bus services might, alone, determine the purchase of a property for private occupation or conversion to office premises. It has no place in schedules of condition or for dilapidation. On the other hand, small plaster cracks are unlikely to trouble a purchaser but they must be carefully recorded, photographed and 'tell-tales' or other movement detectors fitted if judged necessary when any schedule of condition is being taken.

When you have completed your report, it is important that you obtain the agreement of both parties. In the case of a schedule of condition taken before piling or underpinning, one party will be the contractor carrying out the work or his employer and the other party will be the owner of the property inspected. If taken before a lease, one party will be the owner and the other will be the prospective lessee. In the latter case, the schedule is often annexed to the lease for record purposes.

If one party objects to some part of your report, the only practical way to get a consensus is to examine the disputed items on site with all present. If agreement is still impossible you must stick to your professional view. Disagreement is not common but, when it does occur, it tends to concern itself with aspects which are not immediately obvious (e.g. wall slightly out of plumb or the beginnings of beetle attack).

The chances of disagreement between the parties is much greater in the case of dilapidations when your report can be readily translated into cash outlay on the part of one side or another. Points to bear in mind:

❑ You will normally be acting for only one party although it is not unknown for two parties to agree to accept your report in advance (in that case it is technically known as an 'appraisement').
❑ Your report will have financial consequences for one side and may be produced in court, so be certain and assume nothing.
❑ Although you are acting for one party, your report must be fair and reasonable to both; if your opinion is represented, it must be obvious that it is your opinion and not fact.

## 5.3.4   Repair

A property may be in a bad state of repair for various reasons:

❑ Neglect
❑ Fair wear and tear
❑ Inherent defects
❑ Miscellaneous factors

It is particularly important to identify the first reason when dealing with schedules for dilapidation, but you should indicate the cause as far as you can ascertain whenever you note the condition of any portion of the property.

Fair wear and tear may be described as the natural process of ageing of materials, construction and finishes, having regard to the degree of use it is reasonable to expect them to endure. Consideration must be given to location. For example, it would be quite reasonable to expect a degree of damage to hardwood flooring in a domestic dining room due to foot traffic and movement of furniture over a period of years. Scratching and a very gradual wearing down of the surface, greater in some places than in others, would be expected. However, if such a dining room was found to be deeply pitted and badly scored after a similar amount of time, it would clearly be unacceptable and not fair wear and tear. It might take some investigation to decide whether the cause was gross neglect or miscellaneous factors. It would be important to make the distinction.

Inherent defects may be caused by defective basic construction and/ or faulty materials. They may also be original design faults or bad construction. Yet again, they may be due to incompetent rectification of previous defects. The great problem here is that the defects may be hidden so that only the symptoms, not the causes, are visible. Once again, great care must be taken to identify and separate inherent defects from neglect. The presence of a damp patch, for example, may indicate an inherent defect such as a defective damp proof course or it may be due to neglect – condensation, blocked drain gulley, earth piled over damp proof course, leaking gutter and so on.

Miscellaneous factors is a term which encompasses all causes of defects other than those already considered. Among common factors are vandalism, mining subsidence, storms and fire (although it must be noted that fire is often the result of one of the other causes of defects such as a lack of maintenance of electrical wiring).

As well as identifying the basic cause, you must grade the condition of each element in accordance with a scale which you should indicate at the beginning of the report.

All these items may be the responsibility of the tenant, depending upon the precise terms of the lease.

## 5.3.5   The report

The format of the report will be seen to follow closely the inspection report (Section 5.2) and, to avoid needless repetition, reference will be made to that format as appropriate.

If you are preparing a schedule for dilapidation you must clearly show the items which are the tenant's responsibility. In the format which follows, it is suggested that you do this by marking the letter 'T' in the margin opposite the appropriate item. When preparing this report you should inform yourself of the repairing covenants of the lease (if applicable) and of local custom in maintenance and repairs.

# SCHEDULE OF CONDITION (DILAPIDATION) REPORT FORMAT

## Client
## Address of property
## Schedule of condition/schedule for dilapidation [*omit as appropriate*]
## Date of inspection
## Date of report

### Table of contents

**1   Introduction**
In accordance with your instructions of the [*insert date*], I have prepared my schedule of condition/schedule for dilapidation [*omit as appropriate*] on the above property.

**2   Terms of reference** [*include items as appropriate*]

2.1   This report embraces schedule of condition only of the property.

2.2   This report embraces schedule for dilapidation only of the property.

2.3   It has not been possible to inspect the following parts of the property:
[*list the parts you have been unable to inspect but beware that in this type of report particularly, you must have a very good reason indeed if you do not inspect any portion. You must state the reasons very clearly.*]

2.4   Your instructions are to confine my inspection to the following parts of the property:
[*list the portions you have been instructed to inspect*]

2.5   In describing the condition of the various elements, notes will be made of the cause of defects (if ascertainable) under one or more of the following heads:
Neglect (lack of proper maintenance and wilful damage)
Fair wear and tear (normal expected ageing)
Inherent defects (faults due to design, materials or construction)

Miscellaneous factors (all other causes including vandalism, storms, fire).

2.6 The state of repair of construction and finishes will be graded under one of the following classifications:
Excellent (no work required)
Well maintained (little work required)
Fair (some work required)
Poor (a great deal of work required)
Very poor (complete replacement required).

2.7 [*Referring to dilapidation for leases only*]
Items which are tenant's responsibility are indicated by the letter 'T' in the margin.

**3 Location of property** [*include items as appropriate*]

3.1 [*Describe nearby streams, rivers or watercourses*]

3.2 [*Various ownerships and uses of adjoining land or property*]

**4 Mining** [*describe the situation*]

**5 Exterior of building** [*include items as appropriate*]

5.1 Roof [*as Section 5.2 format*]

5.2 Walls [*as Section 5.2 format*]

5.3 Rainwater pipes [*as Section 5.2 format*]

5.4 Windows [*as Section 5.2 format*]

5.5 Doors [*as Section 5.2 format*]

**6 Interior of building** [*include items as appropriate*]

6.1 Basement [*as Section 5.2 format*]

6.2 Ground floor [*as Section 5.2 format*]

6.3 First floor [*as Section 5.2 format*]
etc.

6.4 Roof space [*as Section 5.2 format*]

6.5 Services [*as Section 5.2 format*]

**7 Outbuildings** [*include items as appropriate*]
[*as 5.2 format*]

**8 Surroundings within curtilage** [*include items as appropriate*]
[*as 5.2 format*]

**9  Conclusions** [*include items as appropriate*]

9.1   The inspections of the following consultant[s] has [have] been
incorporated in this report:
   Structural engineer
   Electrical engineer
   Heating, ventilation and mechanical engineer
   Timber rot and infestation specialist
   Acoustic engineer
   Fire brigade.

9.2   **General structural condition**
[*Describe the general structural condition, including particular
reference to any items giving cause for concern even if already
noted in the main section of the report.*]

9.3   **General condition of finishes**
The general condition of the finishes may be classified as
excellent/well maintained/fair/poor/very poor [*omit as appropriate*].

9.4   **Weathertight condition**
[*Describe areas suffering from ingress of damp, including
defective damp proof courses, and which require immediate
attention.*]

9.5   **General remarks**
[*Include any particular problems or features in the building and
curtilage as a whole; keep as brief as possible.*]

# 5.4   Investigation of defects

## 5.4.1   General

The investigation of defects in building calls for particular skill and
care. It is a specialised job often requiring the use of consultants and
certainly requiring a high degree of knowledge and experience on the
part of the architect.

Sometimes the client may ask you to investigate widespread defects
but, more often, you will be asked to investigate a particular defect
which you may well find to be the symptom of more serious trouble. In
the latter case, unless the matter is particularly urgent, you will have to
submit an interim report suggesting further investigation, possibly
involving opening up and testing selected portions of the building.

Points to bear in mind when asked to investigate defects are:

❑ The length of time it has been apparent that defects are present. This could have an important bearing on your client being able to obtain redress. It could also indicate the degree of urgency of your report. You must not allow it to be your fault if the limitation period operates against your client and you should advise him accordingly. Also advise the necessity to consult a solicitor if appropriate. You should be fully aware of the Limitation Acts 1939–80 and the Latent Damage Act 1986.

❑ Your report will form the basis of any claim your client may make. Be prepared to justify in court everything you put in it.

❑ The recipient of a claim for damages will most likely be a fellow architect, a contractor, a local authority, or all three. Carry out your investigation as you would wish them to carry out a similar investigation on one of your buildings.

❑ If you have any doubts about your ability to diagnose the trouble, tell your client immediately and refer him to someone experienced in that particular field.

## 5.4.2 Preparation

After you have received instructions from your client, you should obtain as much information as possible about the building, its construction, maintenance and use. You require information about the following:

❑ Construction and materials
❑ The age of the building
❑ Details and dates of any adaptations, extension and repairs
❑ If there is any regular maintenance contract and the name of the contractor
❑ Details of cleaning procedures
❑ Details of the usage of the building, in particular the type of use and any activities which might give rise to problems (e.g. high levels of humidity)
❑ Type of heating system and frequency of heating
❑ Details of any previous defects and the action taken
❑ The date, as near as possible, on which the present defect[s] was [were] noticed
❑ The degree of urgency your client attaches to your report

Your client will probably be able to supply some sort of drawing if the building is relatively new. If not, you can consult the plans deposited with the local authority. You can approach the original firm of architects who designed the building, for information and also the contractor. You should not do this without first obtaining your client's permission after legal advice if appropriate. Think carefully before approaching the architect or contractor. His response is likely to be guarded. This is only to be expected and you should be wary of drawing any particular conclusions if they refuse to co-operate.

If the building is old, say over 100 years, you may possibly find the plans in the local library or in one of the many archive collections. This sort of investigation involves a good deal of detective work. An initial period of research into the history of an old building will be repaid many times over when you actually carry out your inspection. In addition, useful information can often be obtained, on site, from the people who actually use the building, not forgetting caretakers and cleaners.

When your research has yielded all the information you are likely to get, prepare the equipment you think you will need and proceed with your inspection (see Appendix A).

## 5.4.3   Inspection

It is not intended here to give detailed guidance on the carrying out of a defects inspection. You are assumed to have the appropriate skill and experience. A few points, however, might be found useful. You will be aware, from your client's instructions, the defects of which he complains. The correct procedure should then be followed:

❑ Proceed directly to the site of the defect and make preliminary notes including sketches.
❑ Carry out a general quick inspection of the remainder of the building inside and out; make brief notes of any other potentially serious defects you see.
❑ Return to the site of the primary investigation and inspect thoroughly.
❑ If you are in doubt about the cause, seek immediate instructions (or submit an interim report) to open up the fabric and/or engage a suitable consultant.
❑ Do not be hasty in accepting your own or your client's explanation of the trouble.

## 5.4.4   The report

The report should be as factual as possible although, of its essence, your opinion will be the most important element. Photographs with an indication of scale and measured drawings will be essential to adequately describe your findings in a clear way.

Your client will usually require your professional opinion on suitable remedial measures, together with an estimate of cost. Remedial works may take several forms:

❑ Immediate urgent work and longer term measures
❑ A cheap and adequate, though unsightly, measure
❑ A thorough and expensive set of measures to correct the defect and maintain the architectural integrity

The measures you put forward and the measures your client adopts will depend upon:

❑ Who will eventually pay the bill
❑ The type of building
❑ Your client's financial position

If any measures are deemed to be urgent, you should immediately notify your client by telephone and follow up with a confirming letter. In these circumstances, do not wait until your full report is ready.

The format follows. It can be used for making a final or interim report by including or omitting the appropriate parts.

# INVESTIGATION OF DEFECTS REPORT FORMAT

## Client
## Address of property
## Investigation of [*describe defect(s) and state* Interim Report *if applicable*]
## Date of inspection
## Date of report

### Table of contents

**1 Introduction**
In accordance with your instructions of the [*insert date*], I submit for your consideration my report/interim report [*omit as*

*appropriate*] of the investigation of the [*insert nature of the defect*] in the above property.

**2   Terms of reference** [*include items as appropriate*]

2.1   The report is preliminary only and represents an interim view of the situation.

2.2   No opening up or testing of the fabric has been undertaken at this stage.

**3   General description of building** [*include items as appropriate*]

3.1   Use [*describe use: offices, factory, hotel etc.*]

3.2   Floors. The building has [*insert number*] floors

3.3   Floor plan [*describe the general shape of the plan*]

3.4   Construction [*describe construction in general terms*]

3.5   Orientation [*describe for location purposes*]

3.6   Age [*insert age as accurately as possible*]

**4   Available information** [*include items as appropriate*]

4.1   The following drawings have been inspected:
In the possession of the client [*drawing titles and numbers*]
Deposited with the local authority [*drawing titles and numbers*]
In the [*insert name*] library [*drawing titles and numbers*]
In the [*insert name*] archive [*drawing titles and numbers*]
Obtained from [*insert name*] [*drawing titles and numbers*]

4.2   Alterations/extensions [*omit as appropriate*] involving [*describe extent*] were carried out on [*insert date*] by [*insert name of contractor*]. The architect was [*insert name*]

4.3   Type of heating system [*describe*]. Frequency of heating [*describe*]

4.4   Type of ventilation system [*describe*]

4.5   Previous defects [*describe, including dates, extent and measures taken*]

4.6   Date on which present defect discovered [*insert date*]

4.7   [*Describe any other generally relevant information*]

5 **Defect** [*include items as appropriate*]

5.1 **Location**
[*Describe general location of defect in the building, e.g.* 'Fourth floor, office in south-east corner']

5.2 **Visible symptoms**
[*Describe what can be seen in detail, e.g.* 'Damp patch centrally below window cill on south-facing wall. Patch extending from underside of cill to top of skirting, a distance of 500 mm, width of patch 800 mm at cill level and 1220 mm at skirting level. Lines of efflorescence on plaster at each side suggest that the patch has extended to a width of 1250 mm at cill level and 1670 mm, at skirting level. The cill and skirting boards are painted timber and show no visible signs of deterioration.' *Include photographs in this section with measuring lath to give scale*]

5.3 **Oral information**
[*Describe observations made by occupants including any alterations in the appearance of the defect, heating arrangements, ventilation, storage of heavy equipment etc.*]

5.4 **Investigation**
[*Describe the extent of any opening up and what was visible. Include photographs in this section. Describe any tests carried out, by whom and the results. Describe any other investigation*]

5.5 **Consultants**
The [*insert name*] consultant examined/carried out tests on [*omit as appropriate*] the [*describe*]. The results were: [*describe the results*].

5.6 **Further investigations**
5.6.1 It was deemed advisable to carry out further investigations to establish the cause of the defect[s]. The investigations consisted of [*describe the location, extent and results of the further investigations including photographs*].
5.6.2 My investigations [*add if applicable* and those of the [*insert name*] consultant] have been completed.
5.6.3 It is considered that all necessary investigations have been completed.
5.6.4 It is considered that further extensive [*omit or include as appropriate*] investigations are required to determine the precise cause of the defect.
5.6.5 It is considered that the following consultants should be engaged to carry out investigations and testing: [*list the consultants required*].

*5.6.6* The following parts of the building fabric should be opened up for inspection:
[*list the parts you consider should be opened up*].

**6 Conclusions** [*include items as appropriate*]

6.1 **Cause**

*6.1.1* In my opinion [*add if applicable* and that of the [*insert name*] consultant] the cause of the defect is [*state the cause as precisely as possible*].

*6.1.2* In my opinion the cause of the defect cannot be stated with any certainty at this stage.

*6.1.3* In my opinion the cause of the defect is one of the following:
[*list possible causes*].

I suggest that further investigations, including opening up of the building fabric and possibly the engagement of consultants should be carried out before precise conclusions can be reached.

*6.1.4* It is clear that the defect[s] is [are] far more extensive than originally thought [*describe extent*].

6.2 **Remedial work**

*6.2.1* It is advised that the following remedial works should be carried out:
[*describe in fairly precise terms but stop short of anything resembling a specification*].

*6.2.2* You are strongly urged that the following work should be carried out as a matter of urgency:
[*describe urgent works*].

Until the works are completed [*indicate temporary measures, which may include safety measures*].

*6.2.3* It is not possible at this stage to advise what remedial works are required.

6.3 **Estimate of cost**

*6.3.1* It is extremely difficult to estimate the cost of remedial works. The following must be considered to be for general guidance only. The estimate is based upon rates and prices current at the date of this report. No allowance has been made for inflation and the estimate is exclusive of value-added tax (VAT).

| | |
|---|---|
| Remedial work, including opening up and making good | £ |
| Incidental costs, including removal of furnishings and equipment | £ |
| Further investigations | £ |
| Fees and expenses | |
| Architect | £ |
| Quantity surveyor | £ |
| Other (e.g. clerk of works) | £ _____ |
| TOTAL | £ _____ |

No allowance has been made for interruption of client operations, loss of profit etc.

[*Include as appropriate*]

6.3.2 It is not possible to make any estimate of cost at this stage.

6.3.3 Although it is not possible to make any worthwhile estimate of cost at this stage, it is clear that it will run into many hundreds/thousands [*omit as appropriate*] of pounds.

6.3.4 Although it is not possible to make any worthwhile estimate of cost at this stage, it would appear that the total sum might well be a few hundred/thousand [*omit as appropriate*] pounds.

6.4 **Strategy** [*include items as appropriate*]

6.4.1 In view of the nature of the defects, remedial work should be put in hand immediately.

6.4.2 The remedial work, whilst extensive, can be carried out in phases if desired. I suggest that phasing would be the most satisfactory answer to the problem of defects in this instance.

6.4.3 The remedial work is relatively minor but it should be carried out as soon as possible to avoid further deterioration.

6.4.4 Although the remedial work is likely to be expensive, there is really no alternative but to have the work carried out. Not to do so would result in progressive deterioration.

7 **Instructions** [*include items as appropriate*]

7.1 Your instructions are requested for the following:

7.1.1 To carry out further investigations in the following locations:

[*list locations*].

7.1.2 To carry out opening up of the fabric as follows:

[*list and describe*]

including engaging a contractor on your behalf to do the work.

*7.1.3* To engage the following consultants on your behalf to carry out specific investigations and tests:
[*list consultants by name and describe the work*].

*7.1.4* To prepare detailed specifications and invite tenders from [*insert numbers*] contractors.

*7.1.5* To prepare detailed specifications and schedule of rates for the carrying out of the work and including negotiations with suitable contractors.

## Appendices
A  Diagrammatic floor plans
B  Sections [*if applicable*]
C  Details of specific areas of defects
D  Additional photographs

# 6 Special Reports for Ecclesiastical Property

## 6.1 Scope

The inspection of ecclesiastical property discussed here mainly relates to churches and chapels. They present problems peculiar to their function. A considerable degree of skill and expertise is required in dealing with this type of building. Inspections of such things as vicarages, presbyteries, manses and parish halls should be considered by the methods indicated in Section 5.2. Here, however, the word 'church' should be taken to mean church or chapel.

## 6.2 Procedure

Some religious denominations have their own particular requirements regarding inspections. Others have no specific policy, or practice varies according to locality. For example, a particular diocese may have a permanent architect or surveyor who carries out virtually all inspections, while others employ architects from an approved list.

A feature of the denominations that have a particular practice is that inspections are carried out at regular intervals, usually every five or six years. Where inspections are carried out regularly their purpose is to ensure that the church is kept in good repair and – by highlighting trouble at an early stage – avoid the necessity for extensive and expensive repair and replacement. Normally, the same architect is retained to carry out the regular inspections and also to supervise the carrying out of any necessary work.

When you are approached by the client, you must first ascertain whether you will be required to carry out the inspection in accordance with any particular requirement. If so, you will usually be given a set of printed instructions covering every aspect of your appointment, the investigation and report. In such cases you should carefully consider whether you wish or are able to carry out the inspection on the terms laid down. The report format in this section is designed for those instances where you are asked to inspect without specific instructions regarding the presentation of your report.

## 6.3 Inspections

Churches can vary from the exceedingly old to the brand new. Church authorities normally expect their buildings to last for a considerable length of time, well over 100 years. Churches can be divided into broad groups, for example:

❑ Very fine and important churches irrespective of age
❑ Important churches irrespective of age
❑ Fine churches irrespective of age
❑ Old churches [*i.e. but not fine or important*]
❑ New churches [*i.e. but not fine or important*]

It is useful to place a church within a group because it assists in assessing the degree of maintenance required. For example, a 200-year-old church of outstanding architectural or historical importance will often require intensive care, whereas a 10-year-old church, which is not particularly fine, should require only the minimum of attention for many years to come – routine maintenance in fact.

## 6.4 Report

If your report is to be one of a regular series, it may have a varying format. The very first report you produce will be very comprehensive, a complete schedule of condition in fact. Thereafter, your regular reports may be much shorter, referring to your previous report in respect of items whose condition has not changed since the previous inspection.

The format which follows can be adapted, by omitting certain parts, for use in preparing first or subsequent reports. If you have not produced the first report yourself, you should not take anything contained therein as correct until you have checked it.

# ECCLESIASTICAL PROPERTY REPORT FORMAT

**Client**
**Address of property**
**Regular inspection number** [*insert number*]
**Date of inspection**
**Date of report**

**Table of contents**

### 1 Introduction

In accordance with your instruction of the [*insert date*], I submit for your consideration my regular inspection report on the above property.

### 2 Terms of reference [*include items as appropriate*]

2.1 The last report was carried out on the [*insert date*] by [*insert name*].

2.2 This report should be read in conjunction with inspection reports carried out on [*insert dates of previous reports to which you are referring*] by [*insert name or names*].

2.3 It has not been possible to inspect the following portions of the building:
[*list inaccessible parts such as sealed roof spaces, high spires etc.*]
It is suggested that the following portions should be examined:
[*list parts you consider merit close inspection and note provisions required, e.g. scaffolding, ladders, services of contractor to open up and make good, insurances, etc.*]

2.4 This report is based upon a thorough examination of the site and the buildings and the church maintenance record except where otherwise stated.

2.5 The inspection is visual only, made from ground level and other readily accessible points.

2.6 This report does not include any comment upon the quality of the design of the church or its contents.

2.7   This report does not include any comment upon liturgical suitability.

2.8   This report is not a specification and it must not be used to obtain estimates.

**3   General description** [*include items as appropriate*]

3.1   [*Brief description of building together with notes of features of special importance*]

3.2   **Original architect** [*insert name*]

3.3   **Original consultants**
        Quantity surveyor: [*name*]
        Structural engineer: [*name*]
        Electrical engineer: [*name*]
        Heating and ventilation engineer: [*name*]
        Mechanical engineer: [*name*]
        Acoustics engineer: [*name*]
        Landscape architect: [*name*]
        Others: [*name*].

3.4   **Original contractor** [*insert name*]

3.5   **Principal sub-contractors**
        Structural: [*name*]
        Electrical: [*name*]
        Heating and ventilation: [*name*]
        Mechanical: [*name*]
        Others: [*name*].

3.6   **Subsequent alterations** [*describe*]
        Architect: [*names*]
        Consultants: [*names*]
        Contractor: [*names*]
        Sub-contractors: [*names*]
        [*repeat for every alteration*].

**4   Documents** [*include items as appropriate*]

4.1   **Existing drawings** [*list with numbers and state where they are kept*]

4.2   **Existing photographs** [*list with brief description and state where they are kept*]

4.3   **Other documents** [*list and describe, e.g. maintenance record, brochures, etc., and state where they are kept*]

**5   Inspection** [*include items as appropriate*]

5.1   **External walls, condition**
Material
Construction
Thickness
Expansion joints
Sealing joints
Pointing
Dressing
Weathering
Rendering
Settlement
Tell-tales
Internal plastering
Timber boarding
Damp proof courses [*material, position*]

5.2   **Tower, spire, bellcote, condition**
Material
Construction
Cross
Figure
Weather vane

5.3   **Roofs, condition**
Covering material
Construction
Fixings
Flashings
Linings
Insulation
Structural members
   Material
   Construction
   Fungal or beetle attack
Ceiling material and fixing

5.4   **Rainwater disposal, condition**
Gutters [*types*]
Flashings
Fall pipes
Gulleys

5.5   **Internal walls and columns, condition**
Material
Construction

Thickness
Expansion joints
Pointing
Settlement
Tell-tales
Plastering
Timber boarding
Damp proof courses [*material, position*]

5.6 **Floor of galleries, condition**
Material
Construction
Wall or column supports

5.7 **Internal finishes, condition**
Walls, floors and ceilings
Painting
Varnishing
Staining
Sealing
Murals
Mosaic
Marble

5.8 **Doors, condition**
Location
Materials
Furniture
Finishes

5.9 **Windows, condition**
Location
Materials
Furniture
Finishes
Glazing [*painted, stained or clear glass*]
Glazing bars

5.10 **Installations, condition**
*5.10.1 Lightning conductor*
Location
Material
*5.10.2 Electrical*
Intake position
Phasing
Consumer equipment

Lighting [*type and position*]
Switching
Power supplies and switching
   *5.10.3 Gas*
Intake position
Outlet positions
Ducts
Meter size
Pipework [*material and size*]
   *5.10.4 Water*
Intake position
Stop-tap position
Drain-off cock position
Pipework [*material and size*]
Outlet positions
Ducts
   *5.10.5 Sanitary fittings*
Location
Types of fittings
   *5.10.6 Heating*
System
Fuel
Thermostats
Position of boilers and size
Position of heat outlets
Pipework [*materials and sizes*]
Ducts
   *5.10.7 Burglar alarms*
Type and operation
Position of control
   *5.10.8 Fire alarm*
Type and operation
Position of bells
Position and type of sensors, breakglass points etc.
   *5.10.9 Sound reinforcement*
Type
Position of microphones
Position of speakers
Fixing of speakers

5.11   **Fittings, condition**
   *5.11.1 Bells*
Number
Location
Method of suspension

Ropes
Access
*5.11.2 Clocks*
Number
Location
Mechanism
Access
*5.11.3 Sundial*
Location
Material
Size
Fixing
*5.11.4 Plaques*
Location
Material
Size
Fixing
*5.11.5 Statues*
Location
Material
Size
Fixing
*5.11.6 Monuments*
Location
Material
Size
Fixing
*5.11.7 Altar*
Location
Material
Size
Fixing
*5.11.8 Reredos*
Location
Material
Size
Fixing
*5.11.9 Civory or ciborium [on columns]*
*Tester or Baldacchino [suspended]*
Location
Material
Size
Fixing

    *5.11.10 Sedilia*
    Location
    Material
    Number of seats and type
    *5.11.11 Piscina*
    Location
    Material
    Drainage
    *5.11.12 Easter sepulchre*
    Location
    Material
    Size
    *5.11.13 Rood and/or screen*
    Material
    Construction
    Finish
    *5.11.14 Font*
    Location
    Material
    Size
    Cover
    Mechanism
    *5.11.15 Screens, gates, rails*
    Location
    Material
    *5.11.16 Organ*
    Location
    Material
    Size
    *5.11.17 Other fittings*
    Location
    Material
    Size

5.12   **External drainage – separate or combined, condition**
    Foul
      Inspection chambers [*number, size, location, interceptor trap, air vent*]
      Pipes [*material, sizes*]
      Connection to
        Local authority sewer
        Septic tank
        Cesspool
      Septic tank [*size, construction, outlet, cover*]
      Cesspool [*size, construction, cover*]

Surface water
Inspection chambers [*numbers, size, location*]
Pipes [*materials, sizes*]
Soakaway [*material, size*]
Silt pit [*size, location*].

5.13 **Boundary walls, fences, hedges, gates, condition**
Location
Material
Construction
Size

5.14 **Hard paved areas, condition**
Car parking [*material*]
Paths [*material*]
Terrace [*material*]

5.15 **Soft areas, condition**
Planting
Trees [*size and type*]
Lawn [*size*]

5.16 **Outbuildings, condition**
Use
Location
Material
Construction

6 **Recommendations** [*include items as appropriate*]

6.1 **Maintenance** [*give a brief description of the basic regular work required*]

6.2 **Repair work in order of priority**
*6.2.1* Urgent [*describe*]
*6.2.2* Within one year [*describe*]
*6.2.3* Non-urgent, to be reviewed at the next inspection [*describe*]

6.3 Items which should be kept under special observation [*list and state possible trouble*].

6.4 Parts of the fabric which should be opened up for inspection: [*list*].

6.5 The following consultants should be requested to inspect and submit a report:
Structural engineer
Electrical engineer

Heating and ventilation engineer
Mechanical engineer
Acoustic engineer
Organ specialist
Landscape architect
Restoration expert [*glass, paintings, sculpture etc.*]

7   **Instructions** [*include items as appropriate*]
Your instructions are requested:

7.1   To prepare drawings and/or specifications for the carrying out of the repair work described in 6 above.

7.2   To engage the appropriate consultant[s] on your behalf to carry out further inspections as recommended in 6 above.

7.3   To engage a contractor on your behalf to open up the following parts of the fabric for further examination:
[*list*].

**Appendix**
Diagrammatic plan [*to assist location of items*].

# 7 Proof of Evidence

## 7.1 What is proof of evidence?

A proof of evidence is a written statement of what a witness will say. It is produced mainly for the benefit of counsel who will use it for the purpose of examining the witness before a court or hearing and to assist in cross-examining the expert witnesses for the other party. It is sometimes known as a precognition. It will be prepared if you are to appear as expert witness in litigation, arbitrations or in town planning inquiries. Although a proof of evidence is prepared for every witness, your involvement will usually be in the role of expert witness (i.e. a witness whose opinion is required rather than his remembrance of facts).

This is not the place for a full discussion of the duties and responsibilities of an expert witness. There are many books and courses available for the purpose. It is instructive, however, to consider the duties of an expert witness as set out in *National Justice Compania Naviera SA v Prudential Assurance Company Ltd (Ikarian Reefer)* (1993), TLR 5 March 1993:

❑  His evidence should not be influenced by the pressures of litigation.
❑  He should be unbiased and should never act as advocate for a party.
❑  Facts and assumptions supporting, and detracting from, the opinion should be stated.
❑  He should make clear what matters fall outside his scope.
❑  The expert must say if his opinion is not adequately researched and indicate if the opinion is provisional. He should make clear if he cannot say that his opinion contains the truth, the whole truth and nothing but the truth.
❑  If the expert changes his opinion after exchange of reports, he must inform the opposing side and the court immediately.
❑  All the documents referred to must be provided to the opposing side when reports are exchanged.

The particular position of an expert was re-emphasised in the later case of *Cala Homes* v. *Alfred McAlpine Homes East Ltd* (1995), CILL 1083, where the judge severely criticised one of the expert witnesses for his approach to the task. Anyone can be an expert witness, provided that he has the necessary expertise in the particular area required. Both sides in a dispute will call expert witnesses who support their own particular case. This situation inevitably means that the views of expert witnesses on opposing sides will differ at least in some respects. It is, therefore, vital that your opinion is sincerely held and that you can support it under cross-examination.

## 7.2   Preparation

When you are first approached to act as expert witness, the most important thing to do is to make absolutely sure that you have the necessary expertise. Some experts leave the witness box after being thoroughly humiliated during cross-examination. After you have satisfied yourself on that point, you must proceed to carry out an examination of the evidence and produce a report similar to that outlined in Section 5.4, or possibly Section 4.1, 4.2 or 5.1 in the case of a town planning inquiry. Your client's solicitor or other person charged with care and conduct will examine your report to see if your findings support your client's case. If they do, you will be involved, at some stage, in discussions at which counsel and possibly other experts will be present.

   The purpose of the discussion is so that counsel can examine your findings in detail and make sure that there is no divergence of opinion between experts on your client's side. You will become aware which parts of your report counsel considers most important to the case. Although the barrister will welcome your comments, he or she is captain of the ship and it is counsel's responsibility to chart the course.

   Proofs of evidence for expert witnesses are often prepared by counsel on the basis of the expert's initial report and the subsequent discussion. You should insist on preparing your own proof of evidence because:

❑   It will most accurately reflect the opinions you hold; and
❑   It will indicate how you intend to express them.

If you allow counsel to prepare your proof, you may find that he has (innocently) attributed to you opinions which vary significantly from those you hold. This can lead to delays or embarrassment if you do not receive the proof until the last minute.

# 7.3   Litigation and arbitration

Proofs of evidence for litigation or arbitration are very similar. Before writing, you should find out whether the other party will have the opportunity of seeing what you write. In any case, be sure to use restrained language. Refer to exhibits by description and number [*or letter*]. All the information you produce should be strictly relevant. You will know what is relevant following your discussion with counsel. Remember that the construing of doubtful words in the contract or correspondence is a matter for the judge, arbitrator or tribunal. Do not intrude on their province; it is quite reasonable for you to state what you have assumed the words to mean in arriving at your conclusions.

Although the giving of an expert report is usually entirely the work of an individual, sometimes others may assist in gathering data. It is essential that the role and identity of anyone contributing should be highlighted. The practice is not recommended unless the other contributors are also available for cross-examination.

High Court procedure forbids you from taking your proof of evidence into the witness box. In arbitrations, the procedure depends upon what is agreed between the parties. If you are allowed to read your answers from the proof, the arbitrator and the other side must have copies.

Because of the great variety of possible content, the format for proof of evidence is necessarily short, indicating the essentials.

---

# *PROOF OF EVIDENCE FOR LITIGATION OR ARBITRATION FORMAT*

---

**Proof of evidence**
[*Insert case name*]
[*Insert your name in full*]
[*Put the case name and your own name at the top of each page*]

---

**Table of contents**
[*If you object to taking the oath, put a note at the top of the page that you will 'affirm'*]

[*Insert your full name*] will say:

1 **Qualifications**
   I am [*describe your qualifications, membership of professional bodies, position in, and name and address of your firm*].

2 **Experience**
   I have [*describe, as briefly as possible, the scope of your experience relevant to the matters in dispute*].

3 **Previous involvement**
   [*Describe any previous involvement in the matters in dispute.*]

4 **Investigations**
   [*Describe in detail the investigations you personally undertook in regard to documents and site inspections.*]

5 **History**
   [*Describe the history of the disputed matters, if applicable.*]

6 **Other relevant factors**
   [*Describe any other relevant factors or information you have considered.*]

7 **Opinion**
   [*State your opinion together with clear and concise reasons which led you to take your view. This is the most important section and you should spend considerable time formulating your statement.*]

## 7.4   Town planning inquiries

Most of the earlier comments made in section 7 are applicable to proofs of evidence prepared for town planning inquiries. One important difference is that you will usually read out your proof of evidence and give a copy to the inspector. You will have been called to support or oppose a planning application. Take care, therefore, to make quite clear which you are doing. You may be asked to provide drawings and/or photographs. Be sure to provide sufficient copies for all parties present and make them as clear as possible to the layman by using colour, bold lines where appropriate and omitting all irrelevant details.

# PROOF OF EVIDENCE FOR TOWN PLANNING INQUIRIES FORMAT

**Proof of evidence**
*[Insert the title of the inquiry]*
*[Insert your name in full]*
*[Put the title of the inquiry and your name at the top of each page]*

**Table of contents**

1 **Qualifications**
I am *[describe your qualifications, membership of professional or other relevant bodies, position in, and name and address of your firm]*.

2 **Experience**
I have *[describe, as briefly as possible, the scope of your experience relevant to the matters in dispute]*.

3 **Knowledge**
*[Describe the extent of your particular local knowledge of the inquiry site.]*

4 **Involvement**
I was instructed by *[insert name of your client]* to *[describe your commission]* on *[insert date]*.
    *[Concisely describe your involvement with the subject of the inquiry since your appointment; for example, you may be the architect for the scheme under inquiry.]*

5 **Investigations**
*[Describe in detail the investigations you personally undertook with regard to the inquiry.]*

6 **History of the proposals**
*[Chart the history of the development in regard to planning applications, public participation, interested parties and relevant documents.]*

7  **Special considerations**
   [*Fully describe and evaluate the scheme in relation to architectural, historical, social, environmental, commercial, employment and other pertinent considerations.*]

8  **Conclusions**
   [*Draw together the threads of your statement at this point and state your conclusions firmly.*]
   I strongly urge that the appeal be allowed/rejected [*omit as appropriate*].

9  [*Add your signature and date it.*]

# 8 Health and Safety Plan

## 8.1 General

You should be aware of the Construction (Design and Management) Regulations 1994 and the accompanying Approved Code of Practice. It is essential knowledge and affects all aspects of your work and you should be able to advise your clients not only of what is expected of you but also what the Regulations require of your client.

One of the duties placed on clients is to appoint a planning supervisor in respect of all but the smallest project that is to include construction work (construction work is defined in the Regulations).

No one should seek to be appointed as planning supervisor, nor should they be appointed by the client, unless:

❑ They have demonstrated that they will allocate *adequate resources* to fulfilling the function of planning supervisor in accordance with the Regulations; and
❑ They are *competent* to be planning supervisor – competence requiring a number of attributes, including a knowledge of health and safety as well as designing, always dependent on the type of project being undertaken.

This section assumes you have taken on the role of planning supervisor.

## 8.2 Plan structure

One of the duties of the planning supervisor is to ensure that the 'health and safety plan' is produced. Normally, the appointed planning supervisor will commence production himself.

The plan is produced in two stages – namely a pre-tender plan and a post-tender plan. The latter stage involves the principal contractor appointed by the client in developing the pre-tender plan to indicate how he intends to deal with potential hazards.

The planning supervisor ensures the pre-tender plan is produced. It must contain the information required in Regulation 15(3) and Appendix 4 to the Regulations. The extent and comprehensiveness of the plan will depend to a certain extent on the method of procurement. Therefore the plan for a traditional contract where the design is complete at tender stage is likely to be more advanced and comprehensive than a contract to be let on a design and build basis where much of the design will not have been completed at tender stage.

One of the purposes of the pre-tender plan is to provide information to the contractor when tendering. It identifies the risks, hazards and potential problems but unless a particular solution is required the plan will not at this stage set out how those risks are to be managed. That is for the principal contractor to decide.

## 8.3   Plan character

The plan should not be a standard plan but unique and each project should be considered separately. Ultimately it will be the professional judgement of the planning supervisor that determines what is to be included. There is no need, however, to inform competent contractors about dangers that are normally met on the type of projects that they normally deal with. The plan should not be so detailed that no one reads it. Only essential problems should be highlighted. However, certain matters should always be considered and the headings set out below will assist architects who act as planning supervisors to at least consider all the necessary areas. It cannot be emphasised enough that each project is unique and there may be areas that require consideration that are not set out below. In addition you should refer to Appendix 4 of the Regulations.

# HEALTH AND SAFETY PLAN FORMAT

**Project client**
**Name of the planning supervisor**
**Location and description of the works**
**Type of construction work to be carried out**
**Time scale for the works**
**Date of plan**

**Table of contents**

## 2 Existing drawings

2.1 [*List drawings relevant to demolition, renovation, or erection. As built drawings of structures, plant, services etc. in the works.*]

2.2 Health and safety file [*if existing*].

2.3 Relevant reports [*site investigation, structural surveys, engineer's reports*].

## 3 The design

3.1 Method of design [*including the structure – structural steel, pre-stressed concrete, timber framed – foundations, piling, roof, services such as electrical, gas, heating, plumbing, air conditioning*].

3.2 Information on particular hazards or sequences of work that have not been designed out. [*Include such matters as potential periods of instability, particular methods of erection required, difficult means of access.*]

3.3 Specific reference to risks which have been identified [*such as excavations, scaffolding, compressed air working, use of cranes or other lifting plant, lift installation, high voltage electricity*].

## 4 Construction materials

4.1 Health hazards arising from materials that are specified. They may affect safety or health and should be identified by the designers. [*Include articles of weight causing manual handling risks, activities creating dust, pesticides, ionising radiations, lasers, formaldehyde, styrene, grit blasting, cadmium, highly flammable liquids, noise, hard wood dust, timber treatment, asbestos cement, lead, solvent based paints etc. Reference should be made to Hazard Data Sheets provided under the COSHH Regulations to identify potentially harmful substances.*]

## 5 The site

5.1 Access and egress points.

5.2 Location of site accommodation.

5.3 Location of site storage.

5.4 Welfare and first aid facilities.

5.5   On-site traffic and pedestrian routes.

## 6   Overlap with client undertaking

6.1   Specify any health and safety issue that is raised by the fact the project is located in premises occupied (or partially so) by the client. [*Refer to factory processes, the client's activities, members of the public, the client's staff.*]

## 7   Site rules

7.1   Specify site rules that are to be imposed by the client or the planning supervisor. [*Include such things as working hours, permlt to work systems, emergency procedures, restrictions on methods of construction or types of plant, restrictions on access, noise, dust.*]

## 8   Continuing liaison

8.1   Procedures for dealing with the implications of design elements of all contractors' work as well as design changes made during the contract.

# 9 Use of Consultants

## 9.1 Purpose

Consultants, by definition, are people you find it necessary, or advisable, to consult or to advise your client to consult. They will be experts in a particular field which has a direct bearing on the substance of your report. They will input information or advice which you are unable to provide, at least with their degree of expertise. For example, you may well be able to decide that timbers are suffering from fungal or beetle attack, but only a specialist consultant will be competent to identify the precise nature and extent of the attack and to suggest appropriate remedial treatment. Similarly, a structural engineer will be able to confirm or allay your fears regarding the ability of existing steelwork to withstand additional loading.

The consultants' role is not confined to commenting upon existing structures, of course. Their advice will be needed at various stages in the design of new developments. The range of specialism appears to be increasing and you will have to use your judgement to make the best use of them.

## 9.2 When to use

It is possible to make use of consultants in the preparation of every report discussed so far (with the exception of a proof of evidence, which is essentially a personal opinion; if consultants are required, they will provide their own proof). The extent to which you use consultants will depend on:

❑ The size of the project
❑ The scope of the project
❑ The limitations of your own knowledge
❑ Your client

It is fundamental that, before you use the services of a consultant, you obtain the written agreement of your client. If you are aware – before you prepare your report – that certain consultants will be required, you should obtain your client's agreement before you begin. If, as often happens, you become aware that consultants are required while you are in the process of producing the report, it is sometimes preferable to note the fact in your report (see formats) and, if necessary, produce a supplementary report in due course.

The consultants should be engaged directly by your client in the usual way, although you will recommend them by name and give them their terms of reference. An acceptable alternative is for you to engage them on your client's behalf, i.e. as his agent. Be very precise in formulating the terms of reference for each consultant, otherwise your client may pay more fees than necessary. Decide exactly what expert advice you require and to what extent. You may wish the heating engineer to check the whole of the heating installation, but it would be slipshod to ask him to 'check the heating' if, in fact, all you require is a report on the condition or suitability of the boilers.

When you should use consultants depends ultimately on your own assessment of the situation, bearing in mind the four factors listed above.

## 9.3   Combined or separate reports

You may feel that, if your client engages consultants on your advice, it would be best for each consultant to submit a separate report to your client. You would be quite wrong to take that view unless there were exceptional circumstances. Your client does not want the task of weighing all the reports separately, particularly if the reports contain areas of disagreement. He relies on you to do that for him when you formulate your recommendations. It is your job to co-ordinate the reports of each consultant and incorporate the result in your own report to the client. There is no reason why you should not quote directly from consultants' reports if it is appropriate to do so. You will, of course, note in your own report when particular consultants have been involved in the preparation (see the formats).

To summarise, therefore, it is for you to receive consultants' reports and incorporate them in your own as they apply. You are the funnel through which all the information, including specialist advice, must pass before it reaches the client.

# 10 Back-up Information

## 10.1 Types

Never present a report to your client without having all the back up information you may need. Back-up information is the multitude of documents from which you draw to prepare the report, together with additional information to amplify or explain it. It may take any or all of the following forms:

- ❏ Statistics
- ❏ Local planning reports
- ❏ Regional planning reports
- ❏ Government planning reports
- ❏ Government circulars
- ❏ Design guides
- ❏ Extracts from newspapers, magazines, technical journals and papers
- ❏ Inspection notes and sketches
- ❏ Photographs
- ❏ Design drawings
- ❏ Site plan
- ❏ Location plan
- ❏ Old plans
- ❏ Mining report
- ❏ Test reports
- ❏ Samples
- ❏ Individual consultant's reports
- ❏ Clerks of works' reports
- ❏ Site minutes
- ❏ Your own previous reports
- ❏ Correspondence files

## 10.2 How to decide

It is not suggested that every time you present a report to your client you should take along suitcases full of information just in case they are needed. You would appear, to say the least, to be somewhat lacking in confidence. On the other hand, it is irritating to have to tell your client that you have the required piece of information, but it is back at the office. One solution, of course, is to invite your client to your office to discuss the report. However, it could well be inconvenient; your client may be a board of directors.

Let us assume, therefore, that you have sent copies of your report to your client and, in due course, you visit him to discuss it and answer his queries. How do you decide what to take with you? Approach the problem logically. Go through the report noting down:

❑ Questions you think your client may ask;
❑ The information needed to answer those questions; and
❑ All the other back-up information you have for the report

You will then have a formidable list. Divide the list as follows:

❑ Information required to answer anticipated queries
❑ All drawings
❑ Information which expands the report
❑ Information from which you prepared the report
❑ Additional information which has a bearing on the report

No matter how hard you try, some of the information will appear in more than one category. Some of the back-up information will have been included in the appendices already. Obviously, you need not take that. Experience and common sense suggest that you must take items in the first two categories above to answer queries and explain the report. The other information in the list should be left back in the office. The reasons are that information which expands the report is unnecessary because your client will, if anything, want the report contracted, not expanded. The information from which you prepared the report should be in the finished documents or in your head and any additional information will be rather unwelcome.

## 10.3  When to use

The golden rule is to keep your files and documents closed unless your client asks questions which make it absolutely necessary for you to refer to other documents. Your presentation will be better if you are not constantly referring to circulars and plans. If you start to produce dozens of pieces of additional information your client will be confused and you will have embarked upon a discussion which may never end. It is important that you refer to your back-up information only if your client asks a question which necessitates it. Aim to go in and out of the meeting without opening your briefcase, except to take out a copy of your report.

# 11 Incorporation of Special Clauses

## 11.1 Why?

The incorporation of special clauses in your reports is vital in order to make clear to your client the limits of your terms of reference and, not least, the limits of your responsibility.

Generally, the purpose of special clauses is to exclude unknown factors. For example, it is important to make clear whether or not your conclusions are based on a knowledge of all the facts. If you unreservedly state that it is feasible to erect a factory on a particular site, you are committing an act of incredible folly unless you have investigated everything there is to know about the site and the proposed factory.

Whatever kind of report you produce, it is inevitable that there will be some aspects of which you are unaware either because time is short or because the report does not warrant the expense at that particular stage. You must beware of making careless statements which may result in your client wasting large sums of money. The only way you can guard against this is to state clearly the limits of the known facts upon which your opinions are based.

It has already been stated that, in preparing a report, you should work from facts to opinion. If the facts are not complete you must make the point clear. If your client spends money on the basis of your conditional advice, he will know the areas of risk because you have pointed them out to him in special clauses. He will have little ground to blame you if further investigation causes you to modify your advice.

## 11.2 How?

Special clauses and disclaimers are usually put near the beginning of the report (i.e. under terms of reference). There are exceptions to this general rule and you may find it more convenient and comprehensible to put a special clause in a section of the report to which it particularly relates. An estimate of cost, for example, may incorporate a note regarding the degree of accuracy attained and the areas covered. A good case can be made for arranging certain clauses like that because it ensures that your client has his attention drawn to the clause immediately before or after he read the point to which it relates. A good general guide is to gather all special clauses and disclaimers together under terms of reference and put particular clauses with the topics to which they refer.

## 11.3   Dangers

Little purpose would be served by rehearsing a list of special clauses in this section because all the usual clauses, and a few unusual ones, are included in the formats for easy reference, but in composing your own special clauses, it may be helpful to consider the following as typical phrases with which to begin them:

- ❏  It must be appreciated that ...
- ❏  It has been assumed that ...
- ❏  No inspection/investigation/examination of ... has been carried out.
- ❏  Further inspection/investigation/examination will be necessary before ...
- ❏  Very limited information is available at this stage regarding ...
- ❏  No information is available regarding ...
- ❏  The following assumptions have been made ...

After using the format to prepare your report, it is always advisable to read it through with great care and note whether there are any clauses you wish to include which are not in the format but which are appropriate to the special circumstances of your report.

There are three problems associated with special clauses and disclaimers. The first is that you may miss out an important proviso. The formats attempt to eliminate this danger as far as possible by giving a selection of likely clauses which can be chosen or amended to suit your own purpose. In this respect the formats are 'memory joggers' rather than precise models for you to follow blindly.

The second problem is perhaps less obvious, in that you may guard your position to such an extent that your report could be worthless to your client. The route between the two extremes of reckless advice and advice for which, in effect, you totally disclaim responsibility is tricky. The only thing you can do is to make sure of as many facts as possible and then make clear those parts which are assumed.

The problem of disclaimers goes further. The Unfair Contract Terms Act 1977 considers the question of exclusion clauses and disclaimers in some detail. It is too complex to summarise adequately here and you should make yourself familiar with its provisions. It operates in Tort as well as in Contract.

The effect of the Act was considered by the Court of Appeal in *Smith* v. *Eric S Bush* (1987), a case which concerned a property survey. The surveyors had included a very comprehensive disclaimer in which they attempted to exclude responsibility for negligence. The court decided that the attempt was unsuccessful. The applicable parts of the Act were held to be sections 2(2) and 11(3). Section 2(2) states: 'In the case of other loss or damage, a person cannot so exclude or restrict his liability for negligence except in so far as the term or notice satisfies the requirement of reasonableness.' Section 11(3) states: 'In relation to a notice (not being a notice having contractual effect), the requirement of reasonableness under this Act is that it should be fair and reasonable to allow reliance on it, having regard to all the circumstances obtaining when the liability arose or (but for the notice) would have arisen.'

A degree of uncertainty was introduced by the later case of *Harris* v. *Wyre Forest Council* (1988) in which it was held that the disclaimer in that instance was effective to prevent a duty of care on the part of the surveyor coming into existence in the first place. Both cases were appealed to the House of Lords which dealt with them together ([1990] AC 831). It held that, in both instances, the notice must satisfy the requirement of reasonableness if it was to be effective and that on the facts the requirement was not satisfied. Both cases related to fairly modest dwellings and the situation may vary if large houses or commercial properties are concerned. It is wise to assume that any disclaimer will have difficulty in passing the reasonableness test.

The best method to avoid being caught by the operation of the Unfair Contract Terms Act is to make sure that any disclaimers you include in your report are reasonable having regard to all the circumstances. Be prepared to stand by your professional judgement and where there is doubt, be absolutely honest about it. There is a world of difference between stating that you do not accept responsibility for your own opinions and stating that certain facts are unknown.

# Appendix A   Equipment for Property Surveys

## Introduction

A very common and irritating mistake when carrying out a survey is to take along inappropriate equipment or to forget some items altogether. When preparing to carry out a survey, it is useful to have a checklist of items hanging in a conspicuous place (i.e. on the door of the survey cupboard). Always take more items than you think you will need. Although it would be carrying things too far to suggest that you should take everything on each survey, experience shows that it is difficult to forecast precisely what you will need. A spare tape, a few extra pegs, ranging rods and a torch are always useful.

The checklist which follows includes a brief description of the potential usefulness of each item. The younger and less experienced members of your practice should also find the information helpful.

## Checklist

**Steel tapes**   If great accuracy required, but apt to be damaged and damaging in confined spaces.

**Linen tapes**   Adequate for most work, cleaner and easier to manage than steel tapes.

**Folding measuring laths**   Useful for single-handed surveys, but become loose with wear. Relatively easily broken if made of wood.

**Ranging rods**   Essential for large surveys. Useful for offsets and extending length measurements. Always take more than you think you need.

**Wooden pegs and lump hammer**   Necessary for setting out a grid. Usually $50 \times 50 \times 400$–$600$ mm long.

**Yellow marking paint and brush**   For colouring pegs and making relatively indelible marks for future reference.

**Yellow wax crayon**   For marking stone, brick, concrete, tarmac etc. for future reference.

**Dumpy level and staff**   Perfectly adequate for most property surveys.

**Ladder**   Do not rely on a ladder being available. Take a folding, telescopic or sectional ladder in the boot of the car or on a roof-rack. An aluminium ladder of about 4 metres total length is suitable for most domestic work. For large properties where difficult surveys of the exterior are required, you will probably have to arrange scaffolding or even a mobile platform.

**Compass**   A small pocket compass to enable you to give a reasonable indication of the north point on your sketches. Precise orientation can be fixed later with the aid of an Ordnance Survey map.

**Binoculars**   Useful for examining inaccessible places (e.g. roofs and chimney stacks) from ground level. Magnification of $10 \times 50$ is usually ideal. Greater magnification poses problems because the slightest hand tremor renders proper vision impossible. If you forget your binoculars, the telescope on the dumpy level provides an emergency but unwieldy alternative.

**Spirit level**   Essential in determining whether floors, cills etc. are level.

**Plumb bob**   Essential in determining whether walls are vertical.

**Camera**   Useful for recording details, cracks and general views. Type depends upon your expertise. A flash attachment should be carried for internal work. If you are a complete amateur, an 'idiot proof' camera with built-in exposure meter and range finder is most suitable. Do not ignore the 'instant' cameras which are particularly useful because you know immediately if your picture is successful. Colour film is generally better than black and white because it reveals more detail. If the photographs are likely to be a vital part of your survey or inspection, it is probably worth while having the photographs taken by a professional under your supervision.

**Torch**   It should be as powerful as possible without being too bulky. A rubber-covered waterproof type is generally useful. Some people prefer the type with a handle, capable of being hung or stood in a convenient position to leave both hands free.

**Mirror**   An extremely useful aid, particularly if adjustably fixed on the end of a rod. Glass mirrors give best vision but shiny metal plates are less susceptible to breakage.

**Probe**   A thin steel spike with a wooden handle is used for discovering the depth of rot in timber or scratching away surface grime. A large pocket knife is a good alternative.

**Moulding recorder**   The old system of using a thin strip of lead impressed on a moulding to obtain an outline for transference to paper has been largely superseded by an instrument composed of adjustable rods. It is only necessary if the precise outline of a moulding has to be reproduced.

**Calipers**   Used for measuring thickness of walls etc. when some detail (e.g. architrave) prevents direct end measurement. Not generally essential for normal work.

**Manhole keys**   Varying types available, usually with hooked or keyed ends. A pair of each required.

**Pick**   Useful when the manhole keyhole or bar has corroded.

**Galvanised tube (25 mm dia.)**   About 1 metre in length for applying leverage to manhole keys or supporting corner of heavy lid during lifting process.

**Bolster**   Used with the lump hammer for loosening reluctant manhole covers.

**Drain stain**   Useful for testing runs of drainage and identifying branch discharges. A little goes a long way. Splashes are difficult to remove from clothing and hands.

**Moisture meter**   Useful for giving an indication of the moisture content of timber. They must be used in accordance with the manufacturer's instructions and the results treated with caution.

**Survey board**   Every surveyor has his own favourite type of board. It should not be too big (i.e. it should be possible to hold it comfortably in one hand). A supply of rubber bands and clips for holding down paper, pencils, scale rule and eraser are essential. A plastic flap to cover the board in wet weather is a boon. The type of paper used depends upon the personal preference of the architect and the work to be done. Ordinary A4 bond paper, cartridge paper, squared graph paper and tracing paper are all useful. Special survey books are less useful because they are bulky to fix to a board and they do not easily allow pages to be removed for filing in the appropriate job file. Two or three pencils, ready sharpened, grade HB, are much more serviceable than ball-point or felt-tip pens which do not take kindly, in most cases, to damp paper or being used upside down. Coloured ball-point pens are useful for indicating particular items such as drainage runs.

**Tape recorders**   They are very useful on some surveys as an additional aid but they cannot replace annotated sketches. Remember to take spare cassettes and batteries.

**Dress**   Inspections can involve exposure to dirt, mud, dust, rain, cold and sharp projections. It is essential to make sure that you are adequately protected. It is best to use proper overalls and to wear a cap or beret to cushion the head against unexpected knocks in roof spaces and cellars. Good strong waterproof boots and a pair of gloves with cut-away fingers complete the outfit. In wet weather, outdoor surveys require an anorak with hood and waterproof trousers. Do not wear a scarf or flapping belt, or smoke while carrying out a survey – you will be inviting accidents.

# Appendix B  Sample Worked Feasibility Report

To demonstrate how the formats can be used to advantage, the feasibility report format from Section 4.1 has been developed to deal with a fictitious scheme. The names, locations and estimates of cost are not intended to bear any relationship to real names, locations and estimates.

Although the format has been used as a guide, parts have been omitted, added or altered to suit the particular project and conditions. An example of a pre-printed cover sheet precedes the report. The appendices have been shown in list form only. The example has been kept deliberately short, but it should be sufficient to illustrate the usefulness of the formats in practice.

# FEASIBILITY REPORT

A. Batte
Architect
The Belfry
Badchester BE2 4UR

Telephone: (00) 000010

**Crew Developments Ltd**

**Proposed Office Development, Long Road, Redchester**

# FEASIBILITY REPORT

A. Batte
Architect
The Belfry
Badchester BE2 4UR

Telephone: (00) 000010

22 May 1996

**Table of contents**

## 1 Introduction

In accordance with your instructions of 1 April 1996 I submit for your consideration my feasibility report on the proposed office development, Long Road, Badchester.

4

## 2 Terms of reference

2.1 My brief is to investigate and report on the possibilities for providing the maximum amount of lettable office space on the Long Road site.

2.2 It will be appreciated that the report has been prepared within a very short period of time. It has not been possible to investigate thoroughly the potential of the site. The contents, however, should enable basic policy decisions to be made. A fully comprehensive report can be prepared later, if required, after a closer investigation of all relevant factors has been carried out.

2.3 A full measured survey of the site has been carried out. See the separate report in Appendix F.

2.4 No soil investigation has been carried out and the report is based on the assumption that ground-bearing and water conditions will prove suitable for building purposes without excessive cost.

2.5 Sketch plans indicate possibilities in the broadest terms.

2.6 The following consultants and authorities have been involved in the preparation of this report:

*2.6.1 Consultants*
Quantity surveyor: William Raites
Structural engineer: R.S. Jay
Heating and ventilation engineer: I.M. Hotte
Mechanical engineer: L. Evaytor

*2.6.2 Authorities*
Planning: Badchester MDC
Highways: Rottingshire CC
Drainage: Rottingshire Water Authority
Fire brigade: Badchester Central

5

British Coal: Rottingshire NE
Electricity: RNEEB
Water: Rottingshire Water Co. Ltd
Gas: Rottingshire North Gas Supplies
British Telecom: Badchester
Chamber of Commerce: Badchester C of C

2.7    Information given is, to the best of my knowledge, correct.
       However, it will be appreciated that until formal procedures
       are concluded (e.g. planning application and negotiation
       with other authorities) certain parts of this report must be
       considered as the best information available at the present
       time as a result of personal interviews with the appropriate
       officials.

6

### 3 General information

#### 3.1 Site location

The site is situated on level ground in the commercial centre of Badchester. At present, it is derelict land of some 45 metres frontage and 170 metres deep, approximately rectangular in shape.

The boundaries to north and south are formed by three-storey office premises belonging to Badchester Central Developments Ltd and OK Office Ltd respectively. The western boundary is formed by a broken wire fence with access onto the 8 metre wide Back Road in poor condition (unadopted). The eastern boundary fronts the pavement to Long Road.

The walls of the Badchester Developments building facing the site carry traces of old plaster but appear to be in good condition. The OK Offices building was clearly constructed as part of a structure independent from your site.

The previous building on the site was apparently demolished 8 years ago. Both adjoining buildings are about 15 years old.

#### 3.2 Access

##### 3.2.1 Bus services

The following principal bus services are available from Badchester Omnibus Terminus, half a mile away:

Reeking: every 30 minutes
Rotting: every hour
Fairview: every 10 minutes

7

*3.2.2 Train services*
The following principal train services are available from Badchester Central railway station, 100 metres away:
  London: every 2 hours
  Glasgow: every 2 hours
  Derby: three trains per day

*3.2.3 Private motorists*
The site lies within 7 miles of the M62 motorway, Exit 20. Other readily accessible centres are:
  Manchester: 12 miles away
  Leeds: 30 miles away

3.3 **Employment**
The major employers in the area are:
  Totus Ltd, shoe manufacturers, Reeking. 6 miles south on
    Long Road. Employs 1,200.
  Sheepdip Ltd, fertiliser manufacturers, Reeking. 7 miles
    south on Long Road. Employs 950.
In addition there is a wide range of small employers in the leather trade and agricultural chemical manufacturing industries which employ most of the working population.

8

## 4 Factors affecting the scheme

### 4.1 Rights

Of light: none
Of way: none
Of support: none
Party wall: Badchester Central Developments property
Easements: drainage from Badchester Central Development property to inspection chamber at the extreme north-western corner of your site
Covenants: none

### 4.2 Planning constraints

*4.2.1* The planning officer has raised no objection to the development in principle.

*4.2.2* A previous expired planning permission was granted for an office block on the site in 1981.

*4.2.3* The following planning requirements are applicable to this project:

Storey heights: to match existing at either side, approximately 2900
Number of storeys: 3
Materials: Portland Stone facing to Long Road
Parking: Underground, number of spaces to be agreed but likely to be the whole of the site area
Access: Vehicular from Back Road

*4.2.4* Planning permission has been granted for a 90-bed hotel on a piece of land almost immediately opposite on Long Road. It is understood that the hotel will have good restaurant and conference facilities.

9

*4.2.5* Building lines have been orally agreed as follows:
Long Road: back of footpath
Back Road: 5 metres

*4.2.6* Full planning approval will be required in due course.

*4.2.7* The scheme must be submitted for Building Regulation approval in due course.

4.3 **Drainage**
It is not anticipated that there will be any problems in draining the site.

4.4 **Architectural/historical considerations**

*4.4.1* The site is situated in a designated conservation area and special care will be required at design stage to obtain planning approval.

*4.4.2* The proposals may be considered to be sensitive and opposed by local amenity societies. Consideration should be given to the best way of dealing with possible objections to avoid a public inquiry. Preliminary meetings with the interested parties could be of assistance.

4.5 **Geological considerations**

*4.5.1* Available geological information suggests that no unusual precautions will have to be taken at foundation level, but see 4.5.2.

*4.5.2* The mining position is that workings at considerable depth were in progress under the site in 1987. It is considered that minor ground lowering will take place but, provided adequate precautions are taken, the project can proceed.

4.6 **Statutory undertakings and other services**

*4.6.1* All normal services are available to the site.

*4.6.2* It is likely that the electricity supplier will require a sub-station within the site boundary.

### 4.7 Local authority policy

The project is in accordance with local authority policy for the area which is designated for commercial use on the local development plan. Oral comments from the chief planning officer suggest that the development would be welcomed.

### 4.8 Central government policy

The project is in accordance with central government policy.

### 4.9 Grant aid

It is not expected that any significant amount of grant aid will be obtainable for this project. In view of its location, the local authority may be willing to give some assistance in respect of the Long Road elevation; but such assistance would be counted in hundreds rather than thousands of pounds.

### 4.10 Access

Access to the site is possible at the following points:
  Along the entire Back Road boundary: vehicular
  Along the entire Long Road frontage: pedestrian only.

11

## 5   Design possibilities

### 5.1   Principal planning options
In order fully to utilise the site, it is essential that the new building extends from the Long Road frontage as far west as possible. A problem lies in the site depth which will seriously constrict the amount of daylight because windows are only possible to east and west. It would be possible to overcome the problem by inserting a light well in the middle of the building, but it would result in a reduction in the available floor area for letting purposes. A further constraint is the planning authority's requirement for underground parking. Access to parking will result in a further loss of office space. The alternative, which the chief planning officer might be persuaded to accept, would be ground-level parking, offices along the frontage to Long Road and above the parking. There is no possibility of persuading the chief planning officer to accept a building of more than three storeys high.

There appear to be two practical options:

*5.1.1* Use the whole site with underground parking and light well.

*5.1.2* Use the whole site above ground level with ground-floor parking (if permitted), frontage office space and light well.

### 5.2   Principal structural options
The structural engineer advises that a reinforced concrete basement structure (if required) topped by a structural steel frame is the only suitable system to adopt for either option, bearing in mind the constricted site, the risk of mining subsidence and, therefore, the need to make the building an independent structure without reliance for support from the northern party wall.

12

5.3 **Principal design options**
The requirement to clad the frontage in Portland stone, together with the location in a designated conservation area, suggests a relatively conservative treatment to the Long Road elevation. It will be possible to produce an attractive frontage, well suited to a good quality office development. The light well can be made into an interesting planted internal area with the opportunity to get sunlight into some office spaces.

5.4 **Principal heating and fuel options**
The heating and ventilation engineer has made an analysis of the fuel and heating options (see Appendix D). He is of the opinion that a partial plenum system fuelled by oil is the best option from the point of view of initial capital and running costs and taking into account the great depth but comparatively low heat loss factor.

13

## 6   Estimate of cost

6.1

| Option 5.1.1 | £ |
|---|---|
| Building contract | 11,000,000.00 |
| Additional works (site investigation) | 20,000.00 |
| Fees and expenses: | |
| Architect | 550,000.00 |
| Quantity surveyor | 200,000.00 |
| Other consultants | 90,000.00 |
| Clerk of works | 15,000.00 |
| Total | 11,875,000.00 |

| Option 5.1.2 | |
|---|---|
| Building contract | 8,500,000.00 |
| Additional works (site investigation) | 20,000.00 |
| Fees and expenses: | |
| Architect | 425,000.00 |
| Quantity surveyor | 170,000.00 |
| Other consultants | 60,000.00 |
| Clerk of works | 15,000.00 |
| Total | 9,190,000.00 |

6.2   It should be appreciated that the cost figures can only be considered as very approximate at this stage and for general guidance only. The estimate is based upon the current rates and prices. No allowance has been made for inflation and the estimate excludes value-added tax (VAT).

14

**7   Design team programme**
On the assumption that firm decisions, approvals and instructions to proceed are given by 21 June 1996, the work of the design team would normally take 5 months, producing an estimated start on site on 2 December 1996.

15

### 8 Conclusions

#### 8.1 Assessment

The assessment of options is complicated by the wide difference in price. Option 5.1.1 produces an estimated 27,300 metres of office space at a cost of £402.93 per square metre. Option 5.1.2 produces an estimated 21,700 metres of office space at a cost of £423.50 per square metre. Metre for metre, option 5.1.1 provides the cheapest provision of most office space in accordance with your requirements, but at a high capital outlay. Option 5.1.2, however, is dependent on the chief planning officer's approval to alternative parking arrangements.

Subject to your own financial commitments and advice, option 5.1.1 appears to satisfy your brief more closely and give best value for money.

#### 8.2 Approvals/decisions

*8.2.1* Your approval is requested to option 5.1.1 as assessed in 8.1 above, including the provisional cost estimates in 6 above.

*8.2.2* Your approval is requested to engage a firm of geotechnical consultants to carry out a geological survey of the site at an estimated cost of £20,000.00.

*8.2.3* Your approval is requested to the preparation of outline proposals and report on option 5.1.1.

16

**Appendices**

A  Location plan

B  Site plan

C  Mining report

D  Analysis of fuel and heating options

E  Statistics
Office development in Badchester
Population
Unemployment rate

F  Site survey

G  Photographs of the site

H  Diagrammatic proposals
Option 5.1.1
Option 5.1.2

# Index